Dear Mr. Rosenthal …

Dear Mr. Gaisberg …

An Account of the making of Moriz Rosenthal's HMV Recordings, Compiled from the Correspondence of the Pianist and his Record Producer, Fred Gaisberg.

Bryan Crimp

Travis & Emery

Bryan Crimp.

Dear Mr. Rosenthal ... Dear Mr. Gaisberg ...

An Account of the making of Moriz Rosenthal's HMV Recordings, Compiled from the Correspondence of the Pianist and his Record Producer, Fred Gaisberg.

First published Archive Piano Recordings, 1987.
Republished Travis & Emery Music Bookshop 2009.

Published by
Travis & Emery Music Bookshop
17 Cecil Court, London, WC2N 4EZ, United Kingdom.
UK Tel. 020 7240 2129
From outside UK: (+44) 20 7240 2129
neworders@travis-and-emery.com

Hardback: ISBN10: 1-906857-37-7 ISBN13: 978-1-906857-37-0
Paperback: ISBN10: 1-906857-38-5 ISBN13: 978-1-906857-38-7

"DEAR MR ROSENTHAL..."

"DEAR MR GAISBERG..."

*An account of the making of
Moriz Rosenthal's HMV recordings
compiled from the correspondence of
the pianist and his record producer,
Fred Gaisberg.*

by
Bryan Crimp

First published in 1987 by
Archive Piano Recordings
PO BOX 57
Horsham
West Sussex RH13 7YZ

© 1987 by Bryan Crimp

All rights reserved. No part of this publication
may be reproduced, stored in a retrieval system,
or transmitted, in any form or by any means,
electronic, mechanical, photocopying, recordings or otherwise,
without the prior permission of the publisher.

CONTENTS

Preface & Acknowlegements	iv
Profile	1
Introduction: The Battle of The Blue Danube	8
Chapter One: "Séances" and "grammophons"	13
Session One	*20*
Chapter Two: "A colossal degree of perfection"	27
Session Two	*28*
Session Three	*29*
Session Four	*39*
Session Five	*40*
Chapter Three: "A kind of pianistic akme"	45
Session Six	*60*
Session Seven	*61*
Session Eight	*62*
Session Nine	*63*
Chapter Four: "Very grammophonesque and prepared"	65
Session Ten	*81*
Session Eleven	*82*
Chapter Five: "A kind of triumpf"	83
Discography A: Repertoire analysis	91
Discography B: 78rpm Published Titles	94

PREFACE

Regarding the editing of Rosenthal's letters.

Save for the few exceptions noted in the text all Moriz Rosenthal's letters to The Gramophone Company are written in a generous, copperplate-style longhand. It would have been both presumptuous and sacrilegious to have interfered with his idiosyncratic yet skilled use of English - certainly one comes to relish 'grammophon', 'dont' etc. - and only rarely have I attempted to clarify the meaning of a certain phrase [this being done via the use of square brackets]. The deletion of certain passages - principally because the material was of no relevance to the subject in hand - is indicated by the usual use of dots.

Except on the two rare occasions noted in Chapter Three, all of Fred Gaisberg's letters are addressed to "Dear Mr. Rosenthal". The pianist's approach varied considerably, ranging from "Dear Mr. Gaisberg" to "Dear Friend" though the majority were despatched to "My Dear Mr. Gaisberg".

Record Numbering

Unless stated otherwise all record coupling numbers quoted in the main text are UK HMV numbers. A cross-reference of these UK numbers with American and Japanese record numbers comprises Appendix B.

Acknowledgements

This book would not have been possible had it not been for the generous permission and unstinting cooperation of EMI Music. I am indebted to them for enabling me to present this insight as to how some extraordinary recordings of a legendary artist came into being. Singling out Mrs. Ruth Edge for her unfailing kindness and assistance is only right and proper as she bore the brunt of my inquisition.

I am also indebted to Mr. Richard Warren Jnr., Curator of the Historical Sound Recordings at Yale University Library, Connecticut, America for providing valued information concerning the recordings made at Rosenthal's first session and to Sir John Hall, Bart. and Mr. Malcolm Binns in undertaking to read the manuscript and the resultant helpful advice and suggestions.

Bryan Crimp,
Southwater, 1987.

PROFILE
Moriz Rosenthal (1862-1946)

Familiar as it undoubtedly will be to most piano buffs, the outline of the life and achievements of Moriz Rosenthal needs to be redrawn here in the hopes of fleshing-out the man behind the letters which form the purpose of this book. A gargantuan figure in the history of pianists, Rosenthal has for too long been unjustly relegated to the ranks of a distant keyboard luminary.

Moriz* Rosenthal was born in Lemberg (Lwów) on the 18th December 1862, the son of a professor at the Lemberg Academy from whom he inherited a decidedly philosophical turn of mind. He began to play the piano at the age of eight under the tuition of a certain Galloth, a shadowy figure whose method of instruction apparently placed greater emphasis upon sight-reading, transposition and modulation than the systematic development of a basic technique with the result that the child was soon fearlessly assaulting Beethoven, Weber and the likes without the benefit of a conventional method of fingering. Such an unorthodox introduction to the keyboard seems to have proved no handicap as in 1872 Rosenthal began studies with Karol Mikuli, a pupil of Chopin and at that time Director of the Lemberg Conservatory. Mikuli instilled into his pupils a keen appreciation of tonal beauty and refinement of phrasing, the very qualities, we are told, which made Chopin's style of playing so individual and memorable. Certainly these qualities, in varying and contrasting degrees, are conspicuously evident not only in Rosenthal's playing but in the recordings of two other Mikuli pupils, Alexander Michailowski and Raoul von Koczalski. The young Rosenthal appeared in public playing Chopin's *Rondo for two pianos* alongside his master within a year of commencing studies though no decision concerning the boy's future was taken at this stage.

---
* *Although spelt "Moritz" in most reference books, the pianist preferred "Moriz" and signed himself so in all his letters to The Gramophone Company.*

It was Rafael Joseffy, pupil of Tausig and Liszt and one of the most original pianists of his era, who urged the boy's parents to consider a musical career for their son. It is quite likely that when Joseffy, by all accounts a consummate technician and refined keyboard poet, first heard Rosenthal he recognised the hallmarks of his own playing. The family consequently moved to Vienna in 1875 and Joseffy went to work, providing the teenage Rosenthal with a systematic technical grounding based primarily on Tausig's method. The result was as astonishing as it was rapid to judge from Rosenthal's first public solo recital in 1876, which included Beethoven's *32 Variations in C minor*, Chopin's *Piano Concerto in F minor* and pieces by Liszt and Mendelssohn. After this sensational debut the fourteen-year old Rosenthal toured Poland and Roumania, where he received the first of several royal honours with his appointment as Court Pianist to the King.

In the following year Rosenthal met Liszt, an event long been considered a turning point in his career. A true spiritual father, Liszt encouraged his vast flock each according to their individual needs. Rosenthal remained under Liszt's general supervision for the remaining years of the composer's life, often following the "gypsy priest" on his pilgrimages to and from Weimar and Rome in the company of other acolytes who at any one time might have included d'Albert, Siloti, Lamond and da Motta. As Liszt's pupil Rosenthal made successful appearances in Paris and St. Petersburg though at other times he travelled under his own initiative. In 1880 Rosenthal, already something of a seasoned campaigner, withdrew from public performance in order to study philosophy at the Vienna Staatsgymnasium. Six years later he emerged as man and mature pianist, poised on the brink of the most sensational stage of his career.

Even before the end of the century Rosenthal was widely recognised to be the most astounding pianist of his time, unequalled when it came to technique, temperament and flair. Arthur Friedheim, one of his peers, was of the opinion that Rosenthal (along with Godowsky) could even outstrip Liszt in certain specific areas of technique while the fêted Paderewski acknowledged Rosenthal as the greatest Chopin interpreter of the day. There are even reports that when Anton Rubinstein, generally acknowledged to be with Liszt the great pianistic Deity of the second half of the nineteenth century, first heard Rosenthal he could only exclaim in disbelief, "I never knew what technique was until I heard Rosenthal". (There developed between Rubinstein and Rosenthal an especially close bond; they often travelled together and the young man very obviously modelled himself in the Rubinstein mould during his early years. For all his popular reputation as one of the very greatest of Liszt's pupils, Rosenthal would never fail to remind people of his close ties with Rubinstein.)

Apart from the praise of his fellow pianists Rosenthal also won the admiration of influential critics, not least Eduard Hanslick with whom Rosenthal had studied musical aesthetics at the Gymnasium. Hanslick considered Rosenthal a conjuror, a technician who scorned the most immense difficulties, though it did not prevent him from taking him to task over some youthful 'excesses', in particular the violence of his *fortissimo* playing, defects which he rightly judged would disappear with time. But then Rosenthal's extraordinary technical feats were not of the circus ring but quite obviously rooted in a deep and penetrating musicianship. How else could he have won in addition to public adulation and critical approbation, the unstinting admiration of such diverse composers as Brahms, Goldmark, Johann Strauss II and Tchaikovsky?

Rosenthal's international career had begun in 1888 with a tour of the United States, primarily in a mismatched partnership with the thirteen-year old Fritz Kreisler though both soloists were fortunately able to make auspicious solo débuts. Rosenthal consequently became a regular visitor to America during the last decade of the century though he did not make his British debut until 1895, playing one of his specialities the Liszt *Piano Concerto in E flat*, by which time Rosenthal's life was already set into a familiar pattern, one devoted to incessant travelling and endless acclaim. An interest in teaching appears to have taken root in 1928 when he was appointed Guest Professor at the Philadelphia Curtis Institute while he took many pupils in his old age, of whom the most notable are perhaps Robert Goldsand and Charles Rosen.

As an interpretative artist Rosenthal made an impression both in the accepted classics (including a rôle in the revival of Schubert's music) as well as in the music of his contemporaries - his recording of Debussy's *Reflets dans l'eau* is an object lesson in liquid fingerwork, subtle shading and plasticity of phrasing. In later years, however, he became vehement in his opposition to what he considered the "extremists" of twentieth century music; 'They know nothing and capitalize their ignorance' he once told Ernest Newman. But it is, of course, as an interpreter of Chopin that Moriz Rosenthal is now principally remembered and how he is primarily represented on the two records which complement this book. It is a style of playing that could not have been more different to that of the other recognised Chopin exponents of the time, Vladimir de Pachmann and Ignace Paderewski - proof perhaps that there is indeed more than one road to Rome, though in this particular instance they are all essentially Slavic routes. Rosenthal's Chopin performances are invariably invigoratingly fresh and vital, frequently revealing some hidden melodic motive and always underpinned by an unerring rhythmic sense. Rosenthal apparently cultivated spontaneity through continuous study: he once floored Monteux while they were on tour together by announcing that he was about to embark on a serious study of Chopin's *F minor Piano Concerto* - he was in his seventies at the time. Rosenthal also championed some of the neglected works of Chopin's *oeuvre*, notably the *Allegro de Concert* which was under consideration for recording at the very outset of his liason with The Gramophone Company.

His memory was legendary and, when it came to Chopin, nothing short of miraculous. It is said that Rosenthal intimately knew every single work in Chopin's complete output. Once, in an attempt to get the better of him, someone presented Rosenthal with a solitary bar from a Chopin score which contained not notes but rests. Rosenthal simply asked for the key of the previous chord and promptly identified the work. Yet for all his intimate knowledge of Chopin's scores Rosenthal was not averse to adding personal embellishments. In some instances, as in his celebrated reading of the *Chant Polonaise No.1*, the piece abruptly departs the haven of Lisztian transcription and becomes an awesome and highly personal flight of fantasy. Generally speaking, however, his emendations are less drastic, surprisingly unobtrusive and irresistibly attractive, as for example, in the *glissando* (starting and finishing with a double octave!) in the *G flat Butterfly Etude*.

By the time he came to make his HMV recordings Rosenthal's technique was no longer invincible though it nevertheless remained leonine in its grandeur and elegance. Certainly his keyboard prowess was still attracting unqualified praise in 1934. In February of that year he gave several concerts in London playing at one, by way of an encore, his *New Carneval de Vienne* transcription. *The Times* reported 'a riot of interlaced melodies and rhythms involving every artifice of that amazing technique which almost persuades one that some fairy godmother must have endowed Herr Rosenthal at birth with an additional pair of invisible hands'

This is, perhaps, the opportunity to correct an impression created by the usually reliable Abram Chasins, a great and honest piano connoisseur, in his book *Speaking of Pianists* that at this stage in his career Rosenthal was a has-been. Chasins heard Rosenthal twice around the early/mid-1930s; experiences that were far from pleasureable, the sight of the
> *unhappy and bewildered veteran being sadistically pushed out onto the platform was the most pathetic thing I have ever seen. Not a trace was left of his distinction. Having heard from everyone of Rosenthal's wizardry, of his daring exploits in his prime, I am deeply and frequently haunted by the vision of him as a lost, helpless, and terrified man.*

Ranged against this report, one often cited as proof that Rosenthal's decline was more or less complete by the 1930s, are contemporary reviews and the irrefutable evidence of the HMV recordings while the letters quoted later by no means originate from the pen of a 'lost, helpless and terrified man' but rather the opposite, one only too eager to play both in public and for the gramophone.

In addition to *The Times* review quoted on the previous page it is pertinent to recall the reviews of Rosenthal at work on his triumphant North American tours during the mid/late-30s, in particular a recital given at Toronto's Eaton Auditorium on the 22nd February 1937. The *Toronto Daily Star* reminded its readers that Rosenthal was then the

> oldest touring pianist, nearly 74, short, stout, stooped and prodigious... He wants no pigeon-blue drapes for a backdrop, everything is bare and glaring as a background to a gorgeously colorful sound-scene of master composers, as played by a maestro.

The Toronto Evening Telegraph concentrated on the overwhelming effect of Rosenthal's playing and came to the conclusion

> that the only thing that matters in music is technique after all. Rosenthal's technique is so tremendous, so triumphant, so utterly final - his scales sweep across the picture like flashes of many coloured lightening, his arpeggios leap and ripple and sparkle like water in dazzling sunshine, his chords crash like rock-splitting thunder harmonized in caverns of unmeasured depth, and his smooth legatos roll along like organ music echoing through dim lit cloister and clerestory. The piano is too small for him. His wonderful hands are literally all over the keys in no time - and quicker than that!...But let no one think that this tremendous technique is "soulless". It is the exact opposite...His playing is an amazement.

Even making allowances for the decidedly purple hue of the prose it is quite evident that as late as 1937 Rosenthal was still a major force to be reckoned with.

The HMV recordings of these years tell their own story, revealing with remarkable clarity the qualities which replaced the barnstorming of earlier decades; the lucid tonal beauty and sustained legato phrasing allied to a quite miraculous dynamic palette - which ranged from an occasional *fortissimo* outburst to the most ravishingly delicate of *pianissimo* shades - all of which was placed at the service of a musing, philosophical intellect.

One characteristic which by no means diminished with age, however, was Rosenthal's infamous caustic wit, invariably at its most scathing when it came to the subject of other pianists. In his autobiography *From Piano to Forte*, Mark Hambourg recalls the classic story concerning Rosenthal and another Liszt pupil, Bernard Stavenhagen, a formidable artist but one who chose to confine himself to a very limited repertoire. One evening in the artists' room after a concert appearance by Stavenhagen, Rosenthal joined a clangorous throng of fans one of whom pressed close to Stavenhagen and gushed, "Dear Maestro, would you do me the honour of writing a line or two in my autograph album" adding, in the hope of not unduly troubling the pianist, "Something short will do".

Stavenhagen, somewhat nonplussed, turned to Rosenthal for inspiration. "Well Moriz, what *can* I write which is short and complete?". Rosenthal needed no time to think; "Why not put down your repertoire?" he quietly purred with a sly smile.

Perhaps as a result of his early years with the nonconformist Galloth, Rosenthal's keyboard posture was as individual as his playing. Mark Hambourg would watch Rosenthal play in 'an agony of apprehension' due to the way 'the great pianist lifted his hands off the piano keys, for he was in the habit of attacking them from an astonishing height'. On occasions this approach would inevitably result in a wrong note though to Hambourg this mattered little such was Rosenthal's 'majesty and purity of sound in *cantilene* passages (while) the genius of his personality was overwhelming.' Sir Henry Wood, who conducted for Rosenthal on several occasions, found himself mesmerised whenever he looked at the pianist's hands: 'he held them in such a position that even his clear octaves *looked* as though he were striking chords; and yet nothing except octaves sounded'.

Wood also hints at Rosenthal the idiosyncratic artist - 'a strange personality, his' - recalling how the pianist hated noise of any kind. While on tour Rosenthal would stake out his hotel with infinite care, to the extent of taking four additional rooms if he thought necessary thus ensuring quiet not only on either side but also above and below. Wood also noted that at one time Rosenthal 'had a mania for taking his own supply of drinking water which he carried about in a huge bag of sufficient size to take at least two gallons'.

An eloquent and accurate summation of Rosenthal's art and status appears in a review of a recital the pianist gave in Manchester in January 1921. The reporter was the legendary Samuel Langford, music critic of the *Manchester Guardian* for much of the first quarter of this century.

> *Rosenthal is not a king among pianists in any merely popular way.*
> *He is a purist among the purists of his instrument, and if he makes*
> *a sensational or popular impression it is only because he has so*
> *much technical ability left over after fulfilling the severest*
> *demands of the purist style that he attains popularity in the*
> *hardest possible way. Though there is a look of pleasant suavity*
> *in his general bearing, Rosenthal while playing wears a look*
> *of almost pained fastidiousness, and in the expression of his*
> *playing this fastidiousness is never relaxed. His use of the*
> *sustaining pedal is more scrupulous than that of any other player*
> *in the world...Only very rarely and deliberately did he use the*
> *left pedal to help the flashing and glistening pianissimo, the*
> *diamond clarity of which is the chief ornament of his technical*

> style. These renunciations laid an enormous technical burden upon
> his fingers. Then, if Rosenthal is, on occasion, probably the most
> rapid of living players, there is nothing of bluff or chance in his
> swiftest flights. He is the most sparkling and the most deliberate
> of players.

When Rosenthal died in New York in 1946 it marked the end of one of the longest and most spectacular careers in the recent history of the piano. If the closing decades had not been entirely happy - like many executant musicians Rosenthal appears to have found it difficult to accept the combination of increasing years and waning technical prowess - he must surely have gained some comfort from his work with Fred Gaisberg and The Gramophone Company, recordings which capture him at a stage in his life's work when technical mastery and interpretative genius were perfectly matched.

INTRODUCTION
The battle of The Blue Danube

For all his reputation as one of Liszt's most celebrated pupils plus the fact that he was in a direct, close line with Chopin, Moriz Rosenthal came to the gramophone late in his career. Although the decades of Rosenthal's legendary and phenomenal virtuosity neatly coincided with the infant years of recording - years when he stunned critics, musicians and audiences alike into awestruck disbelief - he chose to remain aloof. He was, no doubt, aware that the primitive acoustic method of recording was quite incapable of capturing the subtle nuances of his playing. Thus it was only with the introduction of the electrical recording process in the mid-1920s that Rosenthal's awesome *pianissimo* playing and haunting tonal palette began to be heard on disc.

Rosenthal was in fact 65 when his first record was published. Recorded on the 8th May 1928 by RCA in America on behalf of the German firm Electrola, then sister companies, it documented on two 78 rpm sides of transcendental wizardry one of his greatest triumphs, a transcription of *The Blue Danube* by one of the many composers Rosenthal counted among his friends, Johann Strauss. Although this recording was naturally issued with his full approval Rosenthal quickly became dissatisfied with his efforts and his dogged determination to "undo" his work caused untold irritation and problems.

The first signs of any rumblings are found in a letter (6.6.29) from Electrola Gesellschaft MBH in Potsdam which reported to its parent organisation, The Gramophone Company at Hayes, Middlesex, that

> *Moriz Rosenthal is not satisfied with the two titles coupled on record EJ 329, and he has requested us for an opportunity to repeat these records which were made by the Victor Company on our behalf... We agree with Mr. Rosenthal and are quite willing to comply with his request, but he informed us that he will not agree to further recordings of his being issued on black label, as long as records of Backhaus, Rachmaninov and others are issued in the red seal category. He is of the opinion that this is bound to prejudice his reputation as a firstclass artiste.*

In its reply (10.6.29) The Gramophone Company concurred. They were of the opinion "that Mr. Rosenthal should be classed amongst the greatest of the front rank pianists" and sought to turn the prospect of his recording with its obviously enthusiastic German branch to world-wide advantage by itemising the type of repertoire it considered best suited to its prestigious, full price Red Label.

> *We note that Mr. Rosenthal may do some further recording for you: if he does, might we suggest that he plays some Liszt, such as the 'Sposalizio'; the 'Spanish Rhapsody' or something from the 'Annees de Pelerinage'. As possibly the greatest living exponent of these brilliant works we should think such records much more worthy of Red Label than the rather insignificant salon pieces he has so far recorded.*

This perceptive advice sadly went unheeded.

Electrola's reply (20.6.29) was lengthy and detailed. Concerning the vexed question of *The Blue Danube* recording it reported that it would

> *have no more records pressed of the existing Nr. EJ 329 (Blaue Donau), a very small number of these records being in stock at present. As soon as these are sold we will cancel the record EJ 329 from our catalogue. We beg you to communicate with the other Branches who have eventually also brought out the record EJ 329 to the same effect.*

The letter also noted that besides re-recording *The Blue Danube*, the pianist also wished to record a further title on a ten inch side which could thus be coupled with a recording of his own *Papillons*, "previously recorded and held in reserve". Presumably this was also recorded by Victor at the same time as *The Blue Danube* sides. (As will become evident Rosenthal recorded his little encore at countless sessions though only two versions appear to have been issued. An obsessive desire to record the piece apparently began on 15th November 1927 in Paris for the Cie. Francaise du gramophone – thus pre-dating his first published record, the troublesome *Blue Danube*.)

Electrola was also pleased to inform The Gramophone Company that Moriz Rosenthal was very taken with the prospect of his elevation to Red Label status though the Liszt repertoire suggestions were referred to only indirectly.

> *The artiste is...quite willing to play more titles, as you suggested with your letter of the 10th inst. but these he would only play against an Advance Payment. Mr. Rosenthal has mentioned in his letter that he has received an advance payment of $5000 from the Edison Company for 3 records"*

For all their considerable musical insight an advance of $5000 for this handful of Chopin titles, recorded in America during March and April 1929, is unusualy high. It is difficult to resist the notion that Rosenthal must have had his tongue very firmly in his cheek.

In reply (26.6.29) The Gramophone Company chose to keep its distance. Rosenthal was, and best remained, a local problem. It was, however, prepared to help Electrola re-record *The Blue Danube* - to this effect The Gramophone Company alerted The Gramophone Company (Czechoslovakia) Ltd. in Vienna on the same day that

> *The Electrola Company of Berlin are anxious to have Mr. Moriz Rosenthal repeat some records which he made for them...He wishes, if possible, to record in Vienna about October 10th*

- but made it plain that a

> *transcription of the Blue Danube is already available under Red Label, and not even Mr. Rosenthal's name could recommend a further recording of this work.*

Electrola's eventual response (7.11.29) carried the information that the repeat of *The Blue Danube* sides plus a coupling for Rosenthal's *Papillons* would take place in their Berlin Studios in either January or April of 1930. For some reason or other the session never took place and EJ 329 remains the only published version of Rosenthal's *Blue Danube* transcription. The Gramophone Company's high regard for their Red Label had obviously been conveyed to Rosenthal who considerably modified his terms which included an advance payment of DM 500 per title - about £25!

Caution, however, remained the watchword; The Gramophone Company were forced to tread a careful path. Basic questions required on-the-chin answers, not least whether the company required records from an artist who for all his prestige displayed pronounced symptoms of being "difficult", and whether these records would prove commercially successful. A brief note of acknowledgement was sent on the 11th November allowing time to assess the situation. The considered reply was written on the 21st November 1929.

> *We think Mr. Rosenthal's terms are quite reasonable, but we are unwilling to undertake a further commitment with a Pianist, in view of the fact that we already carry commitments in connection with a great number of International Pianists of world-wide repute, and the addition of another name would only mean the 'overflooding' of the market for Pianoforte records.*

> *We should, however, have no objection if you made a local contract with Mr. Rosenthal, provided that the agreement you make with him does not call for Advance Royalties and an obligation to list his records.*

> *This artist seems to be eccentric, and has already caused you a great deal of trouble in your endeavour to obtain the few records which you have made with him.*

That surely was the end of the matter; if Electrola and Rosenthal could work together in harmony then nothing would be lost.

But the ghost of EJ 329 was, however, not that easily laid to rest. On 3rd June 1930 Electrola was again writing to The Gramophone Company with the information that Rosenthal had "again complained that his record EJ 329...is still on the market". By now considerations of artistic dissatisfaction had evaporated; Rosenthal was now jealously protecting his status, viewing the entire affair as a personal battle of standing and recognition.

> *Mr. Rosenthal mentioned that he would make the Victor Company responsible for all the damage, as his prestige is bound to be undermined through the issue of his recording under Black Label.*

Not without a hint of panic the letter requested that other territories be asked to follow Electrola's example, namely the withdrawal and "breaking up" of all records held in stock – in Electrola's case this amounted to 45 records. In compliance The Gramophone Company consequently requested (16.6.30) its Czechoslovakian branch in Prague to withdraw Rosenthal's version of *The Blue Danube* from their catalogue (listed as ES 560).

Four months later (29.10.30) Electrola felt compelled to write to The Gramophone Company again.

> *We have before us Royalty Statement for the six months Jan-June 1930, which we have received from your Accounts Department and refer to the exchange of correspondence during June 1929, especially our letters of June 6th and 20th. We had drawn your attention to the fact that Mr. Rosenthal contemplated taking steps against us should we ignore his request to withdraw the record EJ 329 from all our Catalogues and that we had promised him to do so.*

> *Mr. Rosenthal was very indignant when he received from us in April 1930 a further royalty statement for the period 1.7.29 to 31.12.29 and he refused acceptance of our cheque in order not to prejudice his claims.*

> *In order to avoid further difficulties with this artiste we would suggest that we merely keep his account credited with the amounts in question...without sending him cheque or cash for these sums. As you will observe from the Royalty Statement most of the sales were effected in your territory, Overseas and Czecho-Slovakia.*

> *We would therefore ask you again to take up this matter with the various branches with the view to withdrawing the record from the trade and all territories.*

> *Immediately we receive your confirmation to this effect it would be easier for us to remit the amount due to Rosenthal and assure him at the same time that the record EJ 329 has meanwhile been withdrawn from the market. We trust this would settle the matter in a way satisfactory to all concerned.*

In the light of Rosenthal's reputation where money matters were concerned - his dealings with many record companies are littered with queries and misgivings concerning the accuracy of his royalty statements - Electrola must have been more than surprised to find him refusing his earnings from EJ 329/ES 560.

The Gramophone Company was able to reply (13.11.30) that all territories had been requested to stop pressing EJ 329 and that the accrued royalties obviously resulted from stock already held by dealers. It also passed on some information of its own. The pianist was now sending letters of complaint to what he considered to be the source of the trouble -

> *Mr. Moriz Rosenthal has lately been in touch with the Victor Company claiming that his contract has been broken by the records being issued on Black Label instead of Red Label -*

though it was able to assure Electrola that "the artist has no grounds for complaint".

Against such a troubled background, all stemming from the release of *one record*, it is something of a miracle that Rosenthal did eventually embark upon a series of recordings for The Gramophone Company, ironically titles that were envisaged for international Red Label release. That so few of these recordings were published in his lifetime for a variety of reasons, as we shall discover, matters less now that we know so many survived. Recorded by a man in his seventies and with the benefit of that luminous clarity of sound characteristic of The Gramophone Company's solo piano recordings of the mid/late-1930s, they capture, more than any other of Rosenthal's records, the musing keyboard poet and philosopher, a creative artist with more than six decades of music-making behind him.

There is no doubt that during the making of these records Rosenthal tried the corporate patience of The Gramophone Company to the utmost and taxed the long-suffering but always indefatigable Fred Gaisberg, author of the majority of the replies quoted above, almost beyond endurance. That both pianist and producer persisted is indeed fortunate. Some fifty years later and for the first time, we have a new and revealing insight into the art of this very great pianist and, thanks to the preservation of their letters which form the basis of the following chapters, we are given a rare and graphic account of the way these remarkable records were made.

CHAPTER ONE
"Séances" and "grammophons"

Quite how or why Rosenthal came into contact with HMV with the intention of making records for Red Label international release is uncertain. It is unlikely to have been as the result of a personal crusade on the part of Fred Gaisberg - he appears not to have been a great admirer of the pianist's art, mentioning him only twice, *en passant*, in his autobiography. Furthermore Gaisberg would hardly have forgotten his dealings with Electrola in the controversy surrounding Rosenthal's recording of *The Blue Danube*, demands which made him only too well aware of the pianist's unpredictable nature and his penchant for unrealistic demands. In short Rosenthal was, to use Gaisberg's own word, "eccentric".

For his part Rosenthal had possibly mellowed somewhat during the intervening years. Now in his early seventies he must have been well aware that the years left to him on the international circuit were nothing less than a handsome, if well-deserved, bonus. Judged alongside the contrasting styles of his slightly younger peers, notably Rachmaninov, Lhévinne, Hofmann, Godowsky and Schnabel, Rosenthal was already something of an anacronism (albeit a magnificent one) and, as if to emphasise his seniority, the early 1930s saw a new wave of spectacular pianists, spearheaded by Horowitz and Barere, both of whom were at this time making some astounding records. Quite obviously working with what was then the world's leading international record company would serve to enhance Rosenthal's reputation, bolster his prestige and keep his name in circulation once his powers had waned. Certainly in the years since recording *The Blue Danube* Rosenthal had been no stranger to the recording studio. Besides his previously mentioned flirtation with Edison and a brief affair with Ultraphon there was a highly productive liason with Lindström/Parlophone, the company responsible for the publication of the majority of his recordings, including his sole concerto recording, Chopin's *Piano Concerto in E*.

The first sign of any activity within The Gramophone Company is to be found in an internal memo of the 28th November 1933 requesting the drawing up of a letter agreement concerning recording Moriz Rosenthal "during the month of January" 1934. Fred Gaisberg, Artistic Director in all but name of the International Artistes Department, was responsible for repertoire and artist liason. His first direct communication with the pianist, who was due to make several London appearances during February 1934, was via a letter sent care of the pianist's British agent, Ibbs and Tillett. It was open-ended, affording a generous opportunity for Rosenthal to record some of his pet pieces.

16th January 1934

I have just received the programme which you will play in London, and this gives me a guide as to what I should like to have you record. Please do not think for a moment that I want to impose these titles on you, but as you are playing them at your concert, they would be especially welcome by my Company, namely:

Allegro de Concert, Op.46 (Chopin)
Nocturne in E flat, Op.55 (Chopin)
    or as many of the Chopin Nocturnes
    as you care to play
Love's Dream No.3 (Liszt)
Feux follets (Will o' the wisp) (Liszt)
    or
New Carneval de Vienne on Themes by Johann Strauss.

Besides this, we should like to have any of the Chopin Waltzes, such as No.3, 4, 10, 12 or 13.

Perhaps you will let me have your views on this repertoire.

With kind regards,

Yours sincerely.

Rosenthal's reply, from the Park Lane Hotel, London, was both cooperative and investigative.

25th January 1934

Thank you for your charming letter and interesting suggestions.

There are a few important things, which I have to know, before I will submit you a small repertoire, namely:
1) *How long can I play on one side of your disks?*
2) *How short can be a piece?*
3) *From the moment I record with you I would not play for another concern.*
4) *Would you sacrify some amount [pay some money] in order to make free the "Blue Danube", Strauss-Rosenthal?*
5) *The new Viennese Carneval contains about 50% new inventions but 50% of the old ones. What is your opinion about the possibility to play this tremendously effective composition for you, when I state that I played some 2 years ago the old one for Lindström?*

Of course, I have many very striking pieces, which I never played for a grammophone and which I can offer you with full conviction.

With kind regards,

Yours sincerely,

The practical concerns of the first three questions were understandable; the playing time of 78 rpm discs had gradually increased since the introduction of electrical recording and international artists were usually contracted exclusively. In itemising Rosenthal's *New Carneval de Vienne* transcription however, Gaisberg had unwittingly stirred-up a hornets' nest. He was obviously unaware that Rosenthal had recorded this title for Lindström/Parlophone in May 1930 or that it had been subsequently revised. Worse, memories of the troublesome *Blue Danube* (EJ 329/ES 560) had been revived.

Gaisberg, as concisely informative as he was prompt, made it clear that there was to be no financial settlement with Parlophone for the *Vienna Carnival* title which in all probability would remain their exclusive property for ten years from the date of recording.

26th January 1934

Thank you very much for your kind letter of January 25th. I hasten to give you the particulars for which you ask.

Each side of a record will play up to 4 minutes 20 seconds. In the case of shorter pieces, we usually put two small selections on one side, like two Chopin Studies or two small Chopin Waltzes.

Regarding question No.3 we should prefer to have you exclusive during the period that you actively work for us.

With reference to the "Blue Danube" and the "Viennese Carnival", if you have already made records of these it may be as well to omit them from the programme for the time being, until we can clear the situation. However, your repertoire is so vast that there is plenty of new ground for you to cover, without infringing on the claims any other company might have on a particular title.

I shall be on hand at our studio to assist you on the 7th and 8th February at 2 o/c and to help you time the selections. I do not look for any trouble at all on this score.

I have here a contract which I am sending you to cover this work. Perhaps you will look through this and I will be pleased to come down to your hotel if there are any points you want to discuss. The contract is in every way a standard form.

I shall be at your recital on Saturday.

With kind regards, I remain,

Yours sincerely,

Any suspicions concerning the capabilities of the seventy-one year old pianist must have been dispelled by the success of that Saturday recital which seems to have attracted universal praise, perhaps best summarised by Richard Capell's *Daily Telegraph* review.

> *All would-be Chopin-players should have been there to hear. This veteran's art is richer in sheer charm than is that of any of the other great virtuosi. He is too urbane to preach or harangue. He plays to please, but - his nature and style being formed by the traditions and culture of a great civilisation - to please nobly.*

Preparations for the recordings sessions, however, were not progressing smoothly; the contract might well have been "standard form" to most artists but not to Rosenthal. Gaisberg, who apparently dealt with the first flurry of Rosenthal's enquiries after the recital, was a day or so later assuring the pianist by letter that his records would be selling at the standard Red Label price category - "in this category we list such artistes as Kreisler, Rachmaninoff, Paderewski, Chaliapine and Caruso". There was also an amicable lunch together and, during the early days of February, more correspondence clearing further contractual queries. Eventually the way appeared smoothed for the first session scheduled for the 7th February.

It was not to be. A letter addressed to "My dear Mr. Gaisberg" contained some bad news.

6th February 1934

> *This is a very sorrowful episode in my life. I hurt my right thumb and cannot record tomorrow (the 7th Febr.) But I sincerely hope to be able to record a part of the pieces I meant for you, on the 8th February and the remainder in Vienna. Kindly telephone if you got this message.*
>
> *With best greetings and regards,*
>
> *Yours very sincerely.*

It is unlikely that the pianist <u>had</u> suffered an injury, rather he remained obdurate over several points in the contract which had yet to be signed. Rosenthal, insisting on certain unusual and exception emendations and additions, was still beavering away (in no way inconvenienced by his injured thumb) on the evening of the 7th. Not only did he question standard clauses - concerning broken records, Rosenthal complained, "if you deduct such a strong percentage for broken records, etc. where already the income tax takes away about 25%, what shall remain for the unhappy artist?" - but signally failed to fully comprehend what amounted to his basic artistic rights such as "the right to cancel a record whenever I feel it does not do me or the HMV Co full justice". Such were his misgivings that he now wished to completely alter the stance of the one remaining session due the following day.

I propose, I should play one or two records, just to see, how it pleases you, but not for selling purposes. Afterwards we can decide if we can reach an agreement. Dont you agree with me?... I expected only a friendly short agreement, easy to understand, where my wishes should not be incessantly disfigured.

Looking forward to see you at 1.30,

I am yours, very sincerely,

The sessions had yet to start and already Fred Gaisberg was beleaguered. He had little option but to acquiesce concerning many of Rosenthal's demands even to the unusual step of regarding the session booked for the 8th simply as an "experimental" venture, no doubt hoping that the results might justify both the risk and expense of such a venture. And, piling Pelion upon Ossa, Rosenthal insisted on playing his own Bösendorfer piano much against the better judgement of Gaisberg who naturally preferred the Steinway piano used for all solo piano recording sessions in Studio Three at Abbey Road.

After hastily processing the test recordings made on the 8th February - there is no documentary evidence as to what titles were recorded - Gaisberg's misgivings concerning the use of Rosenthal's Bösendorfer were confirmed. He felt compelled to write to Rosenthal on the following morning, only hours before a hastily rearranged additional visit to the studio, now the first "official" session, in an attempt to persuade the pianist to change both his mind and his piano.

9th February 1934

As a result of our tests in the studio yesterday we should prefer you to use our piano for recording if you would not mind doing so.

The Bosendorfer is a beautiful instrument but the other piano matches the characteristics of our recording system and will therefore give better technical results.

With kind regards,

Yours sincerely.

Rosenthal was unmoved and used his Bosendorfer.

SESSION ONE: 9.2.34
                                No.3 Studio, Abbey Road, London.
                                Bosendorfer 24038

2B 6004-1   J.Strauss-Rosenthal: New Carneval de Vienne Pt.1

2B 6005-1)   J.Strauss-Rosenthal: New Carneval de Vienne Pt.2
2B 6005-2)

2B 6006-1)   Liszt-Chopin-Rosenthal: Chant polonais No.1 in G (Maiden's
2B 6006-2)   Wish)

2B 6007-1)   Chopin: Valse No.5 in A flat, Op.42
2B 6007-2)

2B 6008-1   Rosenthal: Papillons (test only)

COMMENTS

Masters for the above were held until 30.7.36 when they were destroyed, the titles intended for commercial release having by this time been re-recorded. Rosenthal's personal pressings are now with the Historical Sound Recordings Library at the Yale University, Connecticut, America with the exception of 2B 6008-1. This item, listed on the original recording sheets as "test only" and thus indicating there to be no intention of commercial release, marks the continuation of Rosenthal's obsession to record this piece. It was to crop up, as a ten inch master, in a further six of the ensuing ten HMV sessions. Also at Yale is an empty record sleeve marked "2B 6004-2". While there is nothing in EMI's archives to indicate that a second take was recorded is it unusual that an alternative take was not recorded particularly taking into consideration that a second take was made for the concluding part of this title.

Where there was a choice of material held at Yale University for the selection of titles for inclusion on the Archive Piano Recordings release devoted to the HMV recordings of Moriz Rosenthal (APR 7002), the indications on the record envelopes, presumably in the pianist's hand, have been taken into consideration. 2B 6005-2 and 2B 6007-2 are, for example, marked "mieux" while 2B 6006-2 is marked "No". The ensuing correspondence gives a further insight into the response of both Rosenthal and Gaisberg concerning these records.

With the session complete Fred Gaisberg's problems were by no means over. For all his advanced years Rosenthal was still globe-trotting and there began the irksome task of getting him to hear his recordings in the hopes of having them approved. By the time the records made on the 9th February were processed Rosenthal was at the Hotel Majestic in Paris. Gaisberg's letter (16.2.34) informing Rosenthal that the records were being sent through the Company's Paris Office crossed in the post with a disgruntled missive from the pianist.

18th February 1934

> *Since the 9th of February I am in Paris, waiting for my records, which were promised for the 12th or 13th but dont come. I cannot stay here any longer than until tomorrow night, where I have to take the "Arlberg Express". If the records dont arrive tomorrow send me new ones or have sent the ones in Paris to my Viennese Address!...*
>
> *Likewise I would like to play some new records in <u>Vienna</u>. Could you give me your consentment...*
>
> *Yours sincerely,*

The records arrived in Paris in the nick of time though it was not until he was back in Vienna that Rosenthal could give them his undivided attention. Gaisberg, meanwhile, not only had to scotch Rosenthal's fancy concerning recording in Vienna but also convey his misgivings concerning the technical deficiencies of the records from this first session. Naturally at this early stage in their relationship he refrained from any mention of artistic merit preferring the pianist to judge for himself. There is, though, no doubting his inference; the recording precluded any prospect of the records being issued.

20th February 1934

> *...Please bear in mind that the records are not as perfect as we could have made them had you played on our Steinway piano. Although your own playing and technique are most excellent, our engineers claim that the Bosendorfer piano has not the crystal clear tone that makes a pure and perfect sound. Consequently, you will notice that on some of the notes, especially in the treble, there are impure and clashy tones. All these imperfections would be non-existent had we used a Steinway for the recording.*

> *Our engineers have made thousands of records and they know exactly what is required from a piano to produce a perfect record. I know that this information will greatly disappoint you because you are undoubtedly very much attached to your Bosendorfer piano.*
>
> *When playing over the records which you took to Vienna, please bear in mind that no matter how good you think they are, they are not as perfect as we could have made them or as we would like to make them.*
>
> *It would be a pity to make your first records in any but the London studio, where we have the latest and the most perfect recording conditions. We would like your debut on our mark to be on the most perfect of records, and this can only be done in London. I am certain that following your great success in Paris and London, you will be coming this way within the next three or four months for a follow-up, and we can seriously consider our recording programme. It is no use rushing these records out when so much depends on the first issue being supremely good....*
>
> *Sincerely yours,*

Rosenthal's initial reaction to the records was surprisingly objective. From a purely artistic standpoint most of them could be bettered though he seems quite untouched by the quality of sound, to the extent of ignoring Gaisberg's concern regarding technical matters by again advancing the idea of recording in Vienna. Rosenthal even investigated the availability of suitable instruments.

21st February 1934

> *...We have one result, as the 'Chant polonaise' came out very well, at least in one of the two discs. The other ones, 'Carneval de Vienne' and 'Valse' by Chopin were occasionally marred and my artistic conscience and care for my name forbid me to send them trough [into] an unkind world. But it is of great value to one, having heard those pieces and knowing now, how I have to proceed at future occasions.*

Now there is one way, namely to try those and other pieces at your Vienna Agency. I have here the excellent Bösendorfer piano, also an excellent Steinway at their Agency and I hope, it will come out nicely. I have nothing to do in the way of concerts in England for very long time, consequently, <u>if you dont want me to come especially to London for this purpose</u>, I beg you to advise your agency to give me all possible support for several séances, where I could play in a dozen of pieces....

Believe me, dear Mr. Gaisberg,

Yours, very cordially,

No sooner had this been posted than Rosenthal appears to have had second thoughts; *could* he do better, might the repertoire have been more carefully chosen?

21st February 1934

I played and replayed with remarkable ease all discs! The result: I hope, to make them pianistically better after the experience I have now. <u>Still I beg you to keep the matrices and not to destroy anything.</u> Could you write me as soon as this letter reaches you, if I can try and play them in Vienna? And if you give me "carte blanche" to play other pieces for the HMV? I would like to play the E flat Nocturne Op.9 No.2, the Allegro de concert, the slow Chant polonais, the Sonata by Mozart (with the turkish marche), the Sonata by Chopin, B minor, the Tarantella by Chopin and other pieces more.

Kindly write me as soon as possible!

Yours, very sincerely,

Infinitely patient, Gaisberg again spelled out the reasons for recording in London and dealt with Rosenthal's repertoire demands which at this stage in the proceedings were hardly realistic.

27th February 1934

>...Both you and I are in accord on the unsuccessful result
>of the recording in London. We must confess that the recording is
>a disappointment, and this in spite of the fact that our London
>studios are the best equipped, not only for piano recording, but
>for all other recording. We have here our best experts, our best
>machines and the best pianos, as well as studios specially built
>for the purpose. This being the case, how can we hope to get good
>results in Vienna, under the handicap of improvised studios and
>recording equipment? My Directors would not approve for one moment
>of our making piano records in Vienna. Our standard for piano
>recording is set so high that it would only be a waste of your
>time and valuable material.
>
>It is against our principles to invite you to come specially to
>London and guarantee your travelling expenses. There is too great
>an obligation and risk here, because again the records might not
>give satisfaction and then we would both be disappointed once more.
>
>Under the circumstances I suggest that we consider the matter
>in abeyance until you come to London on your regular concert
>appearances, when we can discuss the matter further with you.
>In the meantime you can consider yourself perfectly free.
>
>With kindest regards,
>
>Yours sincerely

This letter more than served its purpose, jolting Rosenthal into uncomplaining compliance. The day before it was written, however, Rosenthal was again unburdening himself concerning his first HMV records; personal dissatisfaction seems to weigh oppressively on his mind and he seems aware that his recent demands might well have been excessive, to the extent that he contemplates submitting to the Studio Steinway and coming to London at his own expense.

26th February 1934

> *I cannot picture you my despondency about the imperfection of our discs! Please, <u>dont destroy them</u>, before the new ones, I will make at my next visit to London, shall be perfect.*
>
> *The Steinway of course is an excellent instrument and I fully understand your liking it so much, but it would be good to equalize touch and mechanic, which can be done in 3/4 of an hour.*
>
> *Is it quite impossible to make me come to London in May? And if [I] should pass through London on my way to Buenos Ayres in <u>July</u> would you be there or available?*
>
> *With heartiest wishes,*
>
> *Yours, very sincerely,.*

In his letter of acknowledgement (1.3.34) Gaisberg informed the pianist that he was entirely in accord with the idea of Rosenthal stopping off in London while *en route* to Buenos Aires in "another attempt at the recording". He could be forgiven for thinking that Rosenthal would now be out of his hair for a few months. Back in Vienna, however, Rosenthal was writing again, this time a letter of total surrender. In the face of Gaisberg's uncompromising stand of the 27th February the old man perhaps sensed that his last and finest opportunity to record was about to slip from his grasp.

2nd March 1934

> *There is no question about that the records were not as good as they could be. On the other hand those pieces are much riskier than anything composed by our great classics and romanticists of the literature of the piano. I feel sure that the next time, on your Steinway, all will be perfect.*
>
> *I would not dream to record in Vienna, if you and your directors are opposed to it!*

> *These points fixed, I cannot see, how you can write "In the meantime you can consider yourself perfectly free". We agreed mutally to our contract....I cannot see what happened which should justify this abolition of our agreement!? I did not demand my freedom...*
>
> *Here, whenever this discs (are) privately sounded everybody was delighted and advised me to accept them.*

Gaisberg had no time to become enmeshed in pianistic niceties or even note Rosenthal's change of heart concerning the Steinway. In a brief letter (6.3.34.) he assured the pianist that there was "of course, no question of the abolition of the agreement and we are looking forward to recording with you again in July". This subsequently proved impossible as Rosenthal, contracted for a concert tour of South America, found he had to sail at the beginning of June. His British agents expected him back by the end of September and thought this would be an opportune time to commence recording in earnest.

CHAPTER TWO
"A colossal degree of perfection"

Rosenthal returned from his South American tour slightly later than scheduled but was soon appearing in London - in December 1934 he gave a recital at the Aeolian Hall and in January he "entertained" at the London Palladium - though he did not revisit the Abbey Road Studios until March 1935. While there is no indication that the delay was in any way connected with "temperamental difficulties", it is possible to detect from the resumed flow of correspondence a change of tone in Gaisberg's letters to the pianist, a deliberate attempt to keep himself distanced, inclined more towards matter-of-fact businessman than friendly conspirator. Rosenthal, on the other hand, perceptably warms to Gaisberg, respecting his professionalism and trusting his judgement.

Gaisberg wrote (18.3.34) to Rosenthal, again settled into the Hyde Park Hotel, confirming that the Studio was reserved for Friday 29th and Saturday 30th March and suggesting "the following repertoire: *Mazurkas* (Chopin), *Papillons* (Schumann) and *Lorely* (Liszt)". It is not clear how this repertoire had been arrived at. In the event the second session was rescheduled for the 31st, no doubt to give Rosenthal a respite from what always proved a difficult and demanding task. Of the titles recorded Chopin predominated, though only two *Mazurkas* were tackled; regrettably no Liszt was included and Rosenthal's rather than Schumann's *Papillons* were netted. (If Rosenthal's *Papillons* was to be the pianist's obsession Schumann's *Papillons* was to become something of an *idée fixe* where Gaisberg was concerned. Quite why is difficult to discern: the prospect of Gaisberg requiring all of Schumann's opus 2 - approximately three twelve inch or four ten inch sides - from Rosenthal is as unlikely as his requiring one of its brief scenes.) The appearance of the *Chant Polonaise No.1*, one of Rosenthal's "speciality pieces", comes as no surprise.

For the first session Rosenthal bowed to HMV's wishes and used the Studio Steinway.

SESSION TWO: 29.3.35
                                No.3 Studio, Abbey Road, London.
                                Steinway 0147

2EA 1355-1)   Chopin-Liszt: Chant polonais No.1 in G (Maiden's Wish)
2EA 1355-2)

2EA 1356-1)   J.Strauss-Rosenthal: New Carneval de Vienne Pt.1
2EA 1356-2)

OEA 1357-1   Rosenthal: Papillons

2EA 1358-1)   Chopin: Valse No.5 in A flat, Op.42
2EA 1358-2)

2EA 1359-1)   Chopin: Nocturne No.2 in E flat, Op.9/2
2EA 1359-2)

COMMENTS

    Nothing was published from this session despite Rosenthal's high regard for one of the takes (unidentified) of the Chant polonais (2EA 1355). This was presumably in his own version as elsewhere in his surviving recordings of this title, though the details above are as quoted on the recording sheet. It would appear that Rosenthal found the Steinway impossible for such a demanding and specialised piece as his Johann Strauss concoction and so did not attempt a second side to complete the title.

    The one surviving title - why it was not destroyed together with the remaining sides of this session is something of a mystery - is the Chopin Nocturne (2EA 1359-1). This, the only certain evidence of Rosenthal playing a Steinway during his time with The Gramophone Company, is published for the first time on APR 7002.

SESSION THREE: 31.3.35
                               No.3 Studio, Abbey Road, London.
                               Bosendorfer

OEA 1357-2)
OEA 1357-3)   Rosenthal: Papillons
OEA 1357-4)

OEA 1363-1)   Chopin Preludes: 3, 11, 7 & 23, Op.28
OEA 1363-2)

2EA 1364-1)   Chopin: Valse No.7 in C sharp minor, Op.64/2
2EA 1364-2)

2EA 1365-1   Chopin: Etude in F, Op.25/2 & Nouvelle etude No.3 in A flat

OEA 1366-1   Chopin: Mazurka No.31 in A flat, Op.50/2

OEA 1367-1)   Chopin: "Mazurkas Opp.50/2 & 24/3"
OEA 1367-2

2EA 1368-1   Chopin: Valse No.3 in A minor, Op.34/2

OEA 1369-1)
OEA 1369-2)   Chopin: Etude in G flat, Op.10/5 (Black Key)
OEA 1369-3)

COMMENTS

The recording sheets state that Rosenthal was reunited with his Bosendorfer for this session though this is questionable in the light of the pianist's subsequent objections to all the records originating from both of the March 1935 sessions, as will be seen in the rest of this chapter. The documentation of this session is also unreliable concerning matrix numbering and titling. The discovery of surviving unpublished masters reveals that 2EA 1365, credited on the recording sheets as simply "Chopin Two etudes", actually contains the two etudes listed against OEA 1366-1 which in turn proved to be Rosenthal's first attempt to record the Chopin Mazurka No.31, Op.50/2. The title recorded on OEA 1367 might conceivably have been the Mazurka No.16, Op.24/3.

Once again nothing was published from this session though this time three masters survive: 2EA 1365-1, OEA 1366-1 and OEA 1369-1, all of which are published for the first time on APR 7002. Gaisberg might have held the first two of these titles in reserve with a view to making further takes in later sessions. It is also possible that he held the Chopin Etude recordings in abeyance when he realised that Rosenthal had previously recorded both the Etudes Opp.10 & 25 for Lindström/Parlophone.

Within a fortnight Gaisberg was able to inform the pianist that the records made during the March sessions had been processed.

12th April 1935

> *I am happy to report to you that I have heard all your records and they are most successful. We are sending the samples to:*
>   *Mr. Thallmayer,*
>   *Oesterreichische Columbia Graphophon Agentur A.G.*
>   *Fuehrichgasse No.2*
>   *Vienna 1.*
>
> *He will notify you when they arrive and invite you to his office in order to hear them. Unless they are played on a first-class machine and in a proper room, you will not receive the best impression. Therefore, it is very necessary that you should go to Mr. Thallmayer's office to listen to these records and select the masters.*
>
> *I should have preferred that you had given me authority to select masters, as in this way time would have been saved.*
>
> *I...ask you to let me know as early as possible, the masters which have been selected...Please be very careful to mark the word "Best" and "Second Best" after the records selected...*
>
> *Hoping that you are in the best of health and that we shall have your answer at an early date, I remain,*
>
> *Yours sincerely,*

In his letter (15.4.35) to Thallmayer Gaisberg explained what was required of Rosenthal and noted that a recording was made of Chopin's
> *Waltz in A minor, Op.37/2 [actually Op.34/2 on 2EA 1368-1] but the shell is defective. We are endeavouring to improve this and if we are successful a sample will follow.*

It proved impossible to save this shell.

Having received Gaisberg's encouraging letter of the 12th Rosenthal's curiosity was understandably heightened, though at first he behaved impeccably, restricting himself to the briefest of notes.

26th April 1935

> Since you wrote me, I am eagerly awaiting the discs, but so far in vain.
>
> I am so glad the "Masters Voice" is pleased with them.
>
> Many hearty greetings, from yours,
>
> Very sincerely and cordially,

Delivery of the records was, however, seriously delayed and Rosenthal had to leave Vienna before they arrived. From the Grand Hotel Toplice in Bled, Yugoslavia, he ominously expresses some misgivings concerning the as yet unheard discs before embarking upon a typically idiosyncratic whim.

29th May 1935

> When I played a year or more ago in your world famous Grammophone, it took you a half week to have the discs ready, then you send them to your Agency at Paris. Consequently I hoped for a quick sending to Vienna, this time. I waited patiently at home but no message came from your Vienna representatives. Finally, it was the 1st May, I got an engagement for Milan by wire and had to depart the same night. Another concert at the "Scala" followed, where I played with the Symph. Orchestra of Vienna and had huge success. Now I am at Bled, retained here for some weeks by eminently important financial affairs. I will shorten my sojourn as much as I can in order to hear the discs
>
> My expectations are high! Still there lies a damper Pedal on them. Dont be astonished, when I tell you frankly that I feel not up to my standard when I have to perform on a Grand which does not enjoy preeminence by its keyboard action. When I complained to you about it, you seemed to take it with some reticense and I cannot blame you, as this piano [the Steinway] enjoys a colossal reputation and in many respects by right...But please be assured that I will give my truest and very honest judgement about the discs - this is in my own interest.

> *Now allow me a little diversion. It came to me - from celestial heights or infernal depths - a kind of tango or Habanera, which seems to me, the self flattering author, on[e] of the most original and most catching "Schlapers" (means, effectiv melodies) I know. There is need of a talented english poët, able to compose catching poëtry to my music. It could become the most sensational success of the last times. But you will understand that I could not give it away for a small fee. In the contrary, I would demand a <u>high</u> percentage from the sale and a guaranteed minimum. Where are you in summer? I would - if not to far - come to you and play it to you. Otherwise I will postpone it, until October, where I see you in London.*

> *Now, dear Mr. Gaisberg, forgive me the torture of my english prosa and believe me to be,*

> *Your sincere friend,*

Despite the letter's overall sunny tone Rosenthal's pre-judgement of the records must have troubled Gaisberg; more than a dozen prospective titles on twenty-four masters still remained in limbo while the pianist's "diversion" could only have been a further irritant. Gaisberg appears to have interpreted the letter as if Rosenthal had already given the records a cursory hearing.

4th June 1935

> *I have your letter of May the 29th and am very disappointed that you have not quoted the numbers of your records which you consider successful. Please let me have this information as quickly as possible so that I can proceed with the work of publishing the records.*

> *Concerning your composition, I am certain that if it comes from your pen, it will be fascinating music. I want to hear it played by yourself and I will invite some friends of mine, who are lyric writers, to be present.*

> *With kindest regards,*

> *Yours sincerely,*

If Rosenthal, still in Bled, could do little about the records he did a great deal of thinking about his prospective money-spinning "hit".

16th June 1934

> *I was so glad to receive your friendly and highly flattering letter.*
>
> *Since a week I am in bed and am dictating this lines. In five or six days I hope to be well again and in Vienna, and the first thing I will do, will be to hear the discs.*
>
> *Regarding my composition: Would it not be wise to have also german, french, italian and spanish/South America!/words for it? This means that 250 million of people could be interested in this popular piece. You know how highly I treasure your opinion. Give me your ideas about this important matter. I wonder if you patronize poetry in those foreign languages. Or do you confine yourself mostly to England and America?*
>
> *Hoping to hear from your at your earliest conveniance,*
>
> *Very cordially, with kindest greetings,*
>
> *Yours,*

Gaisberg attempted to extricate himself from any further involvement in Rosenthal's latest flight of fancy.

26th June 1935

> *On my return from the continent, I found your letter of June 16th and sincerely hope you have now quite recovered from your indisposition.*

Regarding the poem to be written for your composition, I must confess that poetry is one of the things I loathe. In fact, when anyone begins reciting on the wireless, I immediately jump up and turn it off! I should think the best thing would be to have only English and German words set to the music.

I shall hope to hear from you regarding your records within the next few days.

With kindest regards,

Yours sincerely,

Rosenthal eventually heard the records in July and wrote an unhappy letter from the Sacher Hotel in Helelental, Baden Bei Wien. (He was still unwell and the letter is again dictated, though the typing is peppered with inked corrections in his own hand.) That Rosenthal's dissatisfaction lay primarily in the use of the Steinway piano comes as no surprise.

<u>10th July 1935</u>

I am extremly grieved that the results of my arduous endeavours in playing the records have had such an unsatisfactory result, in fact there is only one record, the Chant Polonaise by Chopin Liszt, which defies criticism. The others are not flawless. When I played the pieces in London and heard them for a test, they sounded invariably good to me, and I cannot understand how it could be that certain notes sound invariably harsh and destroying the flow of the melodies and the equality of the passages.

I see now that pianos change their intonation during a long sitting and that you have to control them every half hour. In addition I won important experiences about the way to play for the gramophone and I feel sure that I will be able to make the best records possible between October 27th and November 20th, when I will make my English tournée with Mr. van Wyck.

For the present I beg your <u>patience</u> and your <u>goodwill</u> to co-operate with me in order to achieve some triumphant records.

> *To go into details; the Chant Polonaise, which I have marked as the better one, is flawless and belongs to the best records I ever heard. Papillons, the record which I marked as a better one, is possible but by no means flawless and you would do me a great favour by giving me another "hearing" [session] in October, twenty minutes would be sufficient for this. The same applies to the Etude Op.10 No.5 by Chopin. The other records should on no account be published. (No Valse etc.)*
>
> *You will, of course, be very disappointed by these facts but I feel certain that I will play much better records next time, after the experiences I drew from last time.*
>
> *I have been ill for a long time, therefore please excuse my delay in writing.*
>
> *Now about my composition: it was my mistake to speak of "poetry". I meant only <u>words for the music</u> and I wonder if you would undertake the words in another language than English, say German, French or Spanish or if I should take care of this part myself...*
>
> *I remain yours very cordially,*

At this point in the proceedings Gaisberg must have despaired at ever getting records from Rosenthal - four sessions had produced just one approved title - half a record. His reply displays rare patience.

<u>18th July 1935</u>

> *I was very glad to have your letter of July 10th concerning the records. I note there is only one record of which you entirely approve, namely the "Chant Polonaise". As this is only one side, it means that we cannot proceed with the issue of any records, but have to wait until your visit here to re-make the numbers that do not satisfy you. I understand you will be coming in October.*
>
> *Regarding the words for your composition, if you would please send me a manuscript, I would appeal to a song writer to make an attempt at the words. They could be sent to you for your approval.*

With kind regards, I remain,

Yours sincerely,

The always chary Rosenthal decided to hang on to his manuscript as is clear from his reply - which makes no mention of the records.

5th August 1935

After thinking it over, I would prefer, to present you my tune <u>personally</u> and to decide together with you about the next steps.

Thanking you ever so much for your kind interest in the matter,

I remain very sincerely yours,

October was considered a convenient time for another foray into the studios as Rosenthal was about to embark upon a major tour of the British Isles. Come the time Gaisberg, bustling between his office in Hayes and the Studios in London, was unable to attend Rosenthal's opening recital in London.

4th October 1935

I was so disappointed not to see you at my concert! Really!

Am concertizing at the Palladium, also at Edinborough, Glasgow, Manchester, Leeds, Liverpool, etc. After Leeds, the 17th and 18th of October I would be prepared to play records. I have now excellent pieces and we may also discuss my little Tango-Habanera.

I would like so much to record my Blue Danube Fantasy, if you could free this piece from the deadly grip of the Lindströms. Will you try it?

Believe me, yours very faithfully,

Poor Gaisberg! A gentle tickling-off, followed by fresh thoughts of *The Blue Danube* transcription. It prompted the briefest note of acknowledgement promising to get in touch on the 18th October when Rosenthal was due back in London. Two sessions were subsequently arranged for the 21st and 22nd November. A few days before he was due to re-record the titles tackled that March, Rosenthal applied his thinking to the effective commercial exploitation of the popular repertoire and sought Gaisberg's advice.

17th November 1935

> *... Which pieces are most liked by the public ("best sellers")? The long ones like Sonata in B minor (25 minutes!) [i.e. Chopin Sonata No.2] Chopin of middle duration like Scherzi, Ballades and so on (around 10 mins each) or smaller pieces like Mazurkas, Valse, Etudes and and so on (ap. 2-4½ min). I like to come on the 21st with a definite "ordre de bataille".*
>
> *You would oblige me very much by an earliest reply,*
>
> *Yours, very faithfully*

A reply on Gaisberg's behalf was sent post haste. Bearing in mind the troubles so far encountered in obtaining records suitable for publication, there was no alternative but that Rosenthal's repertoire should be kept strictly to the shorter pieces. Curiously, considering Alfred Cortot recorded the work at Abbey Road on the 4th July that year, Gaisberg again raises the matter of Schumann's *Papillons*.

18th November 1935

> *Mr. Gaisberg is in London for the day, but we have told him the contents of your letter of November 17th and he has asked me to write to you and explain that we prefer the recording of short compositions as these are undoubtedly the best sellers.*
>
> *If you make a selection of Mazurkas they should prove very popular. No doubt you will like to add one of Chopin's Waltzes to this programme or possibly such a work as Schumann's Papillons.*

As you know, we prefer to record on our Steinway piano which always gives the best results from a recording point of view, but if you still wish to use your Bosendorfer, will you please arrange to have it sent to the Studio.

We are looking forward to seeing you on November 21st at 3 p.m. at Abbey Road.

As in April, it was found necessary to delay the second session by a day.

SESSION FOUR   21.11.35.   3.00pm
                                No.3 Studio, Abbey Road, London.
                                Bosendorfer

2EA 2561-1)   Chopin: Valse No.5 in A flat, Op.42
2EA 2561-2)

2EA 2562-1)   Chopin: Preludes 6, 3 & 7, Op.28
2EA 2562-2)

OEA 2563-1)   Rosenthal: Papillons
OEA 2563-2)

2EA 2564-1   Chopin: Nocturne No.2 in E flat, Op.9/2

2EA 2565-1   Chopin: Valse No.7 in C sharp minor, Op.64/2

2EA 2566-1   Chopin: Mazurkas No.31 in A flat, Op.50/2 & No.44 in G, Op.67/1

COMMENTS

The change of instrument and Rosenthal's dismissal of all the records originating from Sessions Two and Three, bar one take of the Chant Polonais, ruled out any possibility of "retakes". A fresh batch of matrix numbers was consequently used for these sessions.

Of this fourth session 2EA 2561-1 and 2EA 2562-2 were published as DB 2772. (Persistent rumours than an RCA issue contained four Preludes appear to be unfounded. This might have been prompted by Rosenthal's recording of four Preludes on OEA 1363 - Session Three). The Chopin Nocturne, anonymous in all the archival material but identified in Rosenthal's letter of 30.4.36, was approved for publication but ultimately failed to pass the "wear test". Further technical problems were encountered with the Valtz in C sharp minor, Op.64/2 (2EA 2565) the master of which proved to be defective. The title was consequently repeated in sessions 6 & 7 before being satisfactorily recorded at Session 8. Predictably recording sundry takes of Papillons continued. Again the correspondence indicates that Rosenthal was happy with at least one of the takes recorded in this and the next session though none were ever published.

The recording of the Mazurka No.31, Op.50/2 on 2EA 2566 was to enjoy something of a complicated history. Rosenthal obviously approved this first take for publication though it was never released in the UK and was available only briefly in America. Once again the master appears to have been bedevilled by some technical problem, though quite what is impossible to say. To confuse matters further, this first take contains a second Mazurka unidentified in any paper work or on the record label, the Mazurka No.44 Op.67/1. (See end of this chapter and Session Six.)

SESSION FIVE: 23.11.35.   3.00pm
                                 No.3 Studio, Abbey Road, London.
                                 Bosendorfer

2EA 2567-1   Chopin: Mazurka No.25 in B minor, Op.33/4

2EA 2568-1   J.Strauss-Rosenthal: New Carneval de Vienne Pt.1

2EA 2569-1   J.Strauss-Rosenthal: New Carneval de Vienne Pt.2

OEA 2563-3)   Rosenthal: Papillons
OEA 2563-4) (Res)

COMMENTS

The first three titles were published: 2EA 2567 as part of DB 2773 and 2EA 2568 & 2569 as DB 2836. Gaisberg appears have taken a considerable risk in recording no "safety" second takes in view of all the possible problems involved in the complex processing from wax to metal to shellac; perhaps Rosenthal, in autocratic mood, decided that he could not better his playing and so deemed further takes to be unnecessary.

As he left the Georgian House Hotel for Vienna only hours after the last session, Rosenthal scribbled a hasty note to Gaisberg. He was patently pleased with his work and elatedly planing the couplings of the as yet unheard records.

23rd November 1935

> *I wish you would allow me to play the little Moment musical by Schubert in <u>Vienna</u>, in order to have a pair [i.e. coupling] to the Papillons which otherwise would have to wait until I return. What a pity!*
>
> *I played last time the Chant Polonais and had 2 records from which one was <u>excellent</u>. Kindly couple it with the Valse by Chopin C sharp minor Op.64 No.2.*
>
> *With many greetings,*
>
> *Yours cordially,*
>
> *PS Perhaps the Valse Op.64 No.1, D flat (minute) Valse, would be better than the moment musical? Am just leaving!*

Gaisberg refrained from making a big issue out of the familiar suggestion to record in Vienna.

26th November 1935

> *I have your letter of the 23rd November. I regret very much that we neglected to record a coupling for the Papillons, but I would not recommend this being done in Vienna, because we do not get very satisfactory piano results there; this can quite easily wait until your return in the spring.*
>
> *I will consider your suggestion regarding the Chant Polonaise as a likely coupling for the Valse in C sharp minor, Op.64 (Chopin).*

> *If the Minute Valtz turns out successful, I would be quite agreeable to coupling it with Papillons instead of Moment Musical....*
>
> *Yours sincerely,*

The next stage in the proceedings is predicable - Rosenthal's impatience as he awaits the arrival of test records. He chooses to ignore, as usual, Gaisberg's warning about recording in Vienna.

15th December 1935

> *Almost a month passed since I played my records for you but I did not hear a word about them. When can I see, hear, judge them?*
>
> *About the Papillons! You can conceive how eagerly I await them, as I feel sure they will be a success. Would you allow, I should play a moment musical, or a Mazurka in the Viennese Grammophone? The success will be made by the Papillons and I hope you accept my idea. About the Chant polonais, which I played [belfore last time in London, do couple it with the valse Op.64 No.2 C sharp min and edit [i.e. publish it] as soon as possible, likewise the New Vienna Carneval, the Mazurkas, Preludes and so on.*
>
> *Thanking you in advance,*
>
> *I remain, yours, very faithfully,*

By the time he replied to this letter Gaisberg had been able to appraise the results of Rosenthal's last two sessions.

19th December 1935

> *...I have just played through the records and am straight-way sending them on to you. I hope they will arrive in good condition. I am happy to report that they are the most beautiful piano records I have heard for some time and I must compliment you on their success. I do not think if you played them again 100 times, it would be possible to make finer records. I want you to tell me immediately, which ones we can use for issue; please let me have this information as soon as you hear them.*

> *For coupling, I would suggest the following:*
> > *A flat major Waltz (Chopin)*
> > *Preludes (Chopin)*
>
> > *Chant Polonaise*
> > *Waltz in C sharp minor Op.64 No.2 (Chopin)*
>
> > *Mazurka Op.50 No.2*
> > *Mazurka in B minor Op.33 No.4 (Chopin)*
>
> > *Strauss Waltz Pts. 1 and 2*
>
> *This will leave without coupling the Nocturne which is a 12" record and the Papillons which is a 10". The above list will be quite sufficient to supply the market for the time being and we will hold these two uncoupled titles until you come to London, when the Moment Musical and another selection can be recorded. We have no success with piano recording in Vienna and it would be useless for you to do this work there. The result would only fall below the very high standard which you have attained in London and my Directors would never tolerate this.*
>
> *Will you please answer me this question; Can I put these records up before our Musical Testing Committee for their approval, or must I wait for your acceptance before publishing the records?...*
>
> *Wishing you the compliments of the season, I remain,*
>
> *Yours sincerely,*

Though Rosenthal had still to hear the records, the receipt of such an enthusiastic letter was obviously good news. His understandable impatience was at least tempered by the knowledge that Gaisberg was satisfied with the latest studio work and that the release of four records were planned. Three eventually were published though the intention to couple the *Waltz in C sharp minor* with the highly regarded take of the *Chant polonais* was thwarted by the defective master of the former.

Rosenthal also displays a practical consideration for the duration of sides.

22nd December 1935

The news of the big success my discs have obtained gives me tremendous joy. In fact it is the nicest imaginable Xmas gift to me.

I feel sure that HMV reached a colossal degree of perfection with those discs and I would be happy, if my playing had achieved fullfillament of my wishes. <u>Do kindly send me the discs as soon as possible</u>! I feel they are well nigh perfect and will add enormously to my artistic success.

I will of course wait with my Papillons until April or May, where I will return to London, in spite feeling sure that the effect of this piece is overwhelming and that it seems a pity to wait again 5 months....

It seems to me that the length of both those Mazurkas differs strongly, the first taking 2 minutes, the second more than three minutes. There is a posthumous Mazurka in G major, which takes only a trifle over 1 minute and which I played for your discs and could be added to Mazurka Op.50 No.2...

Thanking you most cordially,

I remain yours, most faithfully,

The fact that the first take of 2EA 2566 did actually contain two Mazurkas while subsequent takes were devoted solely to the one in A flat - the very *opposite* of Rosenthal's final paragraph - has to remain another mystery.

As with almost every other move in this epic the path was to prove far from smooth. It was only after many weeks and several disgruntled letters that Rosenthal was eventually able to hear for himself the perfection, or otherwise, of the November sessions.

CHAPTER THREE
"A kind of pianistic akme"

Most decidedly the New Year did not start well. Rosenthal grew increasingly impatient as he spent the whole of January waiting for the records to arrive; Gaisberg was frustrated by drawn-out processing and production difficulties at the factory, all of which resulted in an increased frequency to the flow of letters between Vienna and Hayes. It was Rosenthal who set the ball rolling.

<u>3rd January 1936</u>

> *I asked today your agency, when they expect arrival of my records and they told me: <u>next week</u>...*
> *I would prefer to hear the records before issuing them...*
>
> *Sending you my best wishes and greetings,*
>
> *I remain, dear Mr. Gaisberg,*
>
> *Yours, very faithfully,*

6th January 1936

> ... *Mr. Gaisberg had gone on a business expedition to Paris for a few days and is expected back at Hayes towards the end of this week...We will show him your letter, and in the meantime we note that you would like to hear the records before giving your approval for issue. As they are expected to arrive in Vienna this week, no doubt we shall hear from you in the very near future...*
>
> *With our very best wishes,*
>
> *Yours faithfully,*

11th January 1936

> *I am so sorry and disappointed, as the discs have not yet arrived! Last time I got them a week after having played [recorded] them. Now 6 - 7 weeks have elapsed! I have to leave very soon Vienna and dont know what to do....*
>
> *With my warmest thanks and greetings,*
>
> *Yours cordially,*

16th January 1936

> *I have just returned from the Continent and found your letter awaiting me. It is very disappointing that the records have not yet been received; they were despatched on January 11th and you should receive them about January 22nd...*
>
> *I hope soon to hear that you are completely satisfied with your records, and with my very best wishes for the New Year,*
>
> *Yours sincerely,*

Growing increasingly discontented Rosenthal resorted to the telegram. Gaisberg, safe in the knowledge that the records had been despatched, deftly deflected the ball back into Rosenthal's court.

17th January 1936

> *We confirm exchange of telegrams as follows:*
> *"DISAPPOINTED GRIEVED SEND DISCS - ROSENTHAL"*
> *"TRANSPORT DIFFICULT RECORDS SHOULD ARRIVE MONDAY - GRAMOPHONE"*
>
> *I have always warned you that it is most difficult and uncertain to send records to Austria in these days. There are many obstacles in the way and that is why I hoped you would let us pass these records here. We are now in your hands and hope that you will let us have an early decision as to whether we can use these records commercially.*
>
> *Looking forward to hearing from you, I remain,*
>
> *Yours sincerely,*

20th January 1936

> *In your letter from Jan 17th you state [to] having warned me that it is most difficult and uncertain to send records to Austria in these days.*
>
> *Permit me to tell you that not the slightest trace of this words and warnings remained in my otherwise excellent memory. Moreover I cannot understand why the Grammophone Co. took 3 weeks to finish and send off the records whereas for a last time it took you only 5 days.*
>
> *Since ten days I am postponing my voyage to Susak (Yougoslavia), where I reserved rooms for myself and my piano and all this, to hear the records. What shall I do now? I must leave the 22nd evening.....*

Sending you my most cordial greetings,

I remain, yours very sincerely,

If Gaisberg, always a loyal company man, dodged Rosenthal's central question as to exactly why it had taken so long to process the records made on the 21st and 23rd November, it is obvious that he felt some sympathy for the old man's situation. In the first of only two letters resulting from his entire dealings with Rosenthal, he addressed the pianist not with his standard "Dear Mr. Rosenthal" but as "Dear Maestro"

28th January 1936

I am very sorry that you had to leave for Yugoslavia before the records arrived. I did everything possible to expedite the shipment and I am informed by the factory that there was no delay and that it is quite normal for shipments to take a fortnight in transit. I know how impatient you were to hear these records and I hope by this time they have reached you.

Hoping that you are in the best of health and looking forward to hearing your verdict on the records, I remain,

Yours sincerely,

From the Hotel Jadran in Susak Rosenthal, still in total ignorance as to how the records sounded, hammered away in an attempt to learn why there had been such a protracted delay. More significantly he decided to cut corners.

2nd February 1936

I was not astonished about the fortnight the records took to arrive in Vienna. But what was rather incomprehensible to me was that the finishing [processing] of my records took 7 weeks!

> *I could not wait any longer in Vienna and went to Yougoslavia for some concerts. But Mrs. Rosenthal heard the records and was delighted. Now, she is a pianist of high rank and knows the whole literature. Having therefore your favourable judgement, based on a wonderful ear for acoustic impression and the pianistical applaus of Mrs. Rosenthal I authorise you to sell a half million of each of my records. Bueno?...*
>
> *Sending you my best wishes and greetings,*
>
> *I remain, dear Mr. Gaisberg,*
>
> *Yours, very cordially,*

This was a considerable coup. At no other time in his dealings with The Gramophone Company (or any other company, one suspects) did Rosenthal permit records to be published without first hearing them for approval.

5th February 1936

> *We are acknowledging your letter of the 2nd February in Mr. Gaisberg's absence, who is laid up for a few days with a cold.*
>
> *We are pleased to hear that the records have arrived in Vienna and that Mrs. Rosenthal has given a favourable report agreeing with our own opinion. As you approve the records we are putting them into production at once...*
>
> *We will show your letter to Mr. Gaisberg as soon as he returns to the office and we know that he will be delighted to hear that you have approved the records.*
>
> *Yours sincerely,*

Having granted permission for the release of these records the next question could be anticipated. (For once, literally speaking, Rosenthal did not date his letter sent from the Park Hotel in Susak.)

(?) February 1936

When will my new discs go into the world?

I wish so much you would give me your most powerful support for my cyclus [cycle] of the 7 historical concerts (from Bach to 1900). I will play seven times [in London] between end of April until May 16th.

I intend to stay in London after those concerts and play a nice lot of pieces derived of those programmes into the discs of HMV. Would the great Grammophone Co shrink from the expense to bring those formidable programmes put together in three or four great papers [i.e. advertise in the national press]? This would create a sensation for the Company and myself...

With my best wishes and greetings,

I remain yours, cordially,

9th March 1936

I thank you for your kind letter from Susak. I am quite alive to your stupendous series of concerts at the Wigmore Hall and will certainly urge our Advertising Department to link up in every way possible.

You will appreciate, however, that in reality we have only two records of yours to offer to the public, namely:
   Mazurka Op.50 No.2) (Chopin)
   Mazurka Op.33 No.4)   "
   Waltz Op.42   ) (Chopin)
   Three preludes, Op.28)   "
and this is not a very imposing list for us to advertise. However, we will do the best we can.

I note that there will be a possibility of making some further records during the period of your concerts and we will make preparations for this as well....

Yours sincerely,

Although approved *Carneval de Vienne* could not be issued as it remained the province of Lindström/Parlophone for whom Rosenthal had recorded the original version in May 1930. This, together with *The Blue Danube*, was bound to crop-up in Rosenthal's reply, written while he was still in Susak.

<u>13th March 1936</u>

> *Let me make a strong appeal to your excellent memory! You asked me a year ago about pieces I wished to play into HMV. I asked you if you were on good terms with the Columbia [actually Parlophone] /Lindström and if you could free my Strauss Fantasias, Carneval de Vienne and blue Danube and you answered you were on best terms and would succeed in freeing them for you. I played then, a year afterwards, the New Viennese Carneval, which is new only for the minor part...This new Vienna Carneval (partly new) seems to be a kind of pianistic akme, and it would be a pity, to resign without trying to get it free.*
>
> *In your list of my pieces, played for you, I miss <u>two</u> which would give an excellent disk: one side - Chant polonais G maj Chopin-Liszt and on the other side Valse, Op.64 No.2 C sharp minor by Chopin. Madame Rosenthal who has an excellent ear and taste was quite enthusiastic about those two pieces. Why do you refrain from selling them? Kindly write me about all those various points....*
>
> *Looking forward to an agreeable letter,*
>
> *I remain, dear Mr. Gaisberg,*
>
> *Yours very sincerely,*
>
> *PS: I would like you so much to give me opportunity to play [record] for you after my cyclus, which finishes the 16th May, from the 19th of May until 30th May.*

In his second letter addressed to "Dear Maestro", Gaisberg broke the news as to why Rosenthal's favoured titles could not be paired for issue.

18th March 1936

>   I thank you for your letter of March 13th and I am taking up the
>   matter of the New Carneval de Vienna with the parties concerned.
>
>   Regarding the two pieces which you say you miss from our list, I
>   regret that the Waltz Op.62 No.2 shows grave defects in the surface
>   which are very disturbing and for this reason we have withheld it.
>   This means that the Chant Polonaise has no coupling for the
>   moment.
>
>   I note that you can record from the 19th to the 30th May and will
>   set aside some dates during this period for you. This should
>   result in a good stock of your records, to carry us over for some
>   time....
>
>   Hoping that you are in the best of health and looking forward to
>   seeing you,
>
>   I remain, yours sincerely,

In quick succession Rosenthal twice begs Gaisberg not to forget the two titles which have his full, unquestioning approval, failing to comprehend that the Chopin *Waltz in A flat* is, to all intents, irretrievably lost.

21st March 1936

>   ...Dont omit the records of the Chant polonais (fore last time)
>   [i.e. Session Two], Valse A flat, Op.42, as they are very <u>brilliant</u>...
>   And kindly reserve one [session] around 10 days for new exploits,
>   after my concerts (say from may 18th on).
>
>   With kindest regards,
>
>   Yours cordially,

22nd March 1936

> *Le Chant polonais is the only <u>pianistically</u> interesting piece
> I played besides the Vienna Carneval for HMV. You would oblige me
> infinitely in coupling the Chant polonais with the A flat Valse
> Op.42 by Chopin. This will prove very interesting indeed...*

Why this version of the *Chant polonais* was not issued we shall probably never know - Rosenthal eventually re-recorded the title in Session Eight. It is possible that the difference in sound between this side, recorded on the Studio Steinway, and any other title, which would have been played on Rosenthal's preferred Bosendorfer, was considered incompatible.

In response to Rosenthal's letter of the 21st, Gaisberg confirmed that he would reserve the studios as soon as he knew the pianist's preference for the time of day, he personally recommending "from 10 to 12 o/c, when everybody is fresh". Rosenthal, however, is mostly concerned with his favourite titles.

27th March 1936

> *Did you get any answers from Lindström...about the Viennese
> Carnaval? Will you do me the favour to couple the Chant polonais
> with the A flat Valse by Chopin? I want both pieces badly.*
>
> *About my playing into your grammophone: I beg you, to reserve
> me the time from <u>3</u> o clock to five or longer. I have then
> time to repeat the pieces at my Hotel and can deliver a more
> consciencious reading...*
>
> *Sending you my best wishes and kindest greetings,*
>
> *I remain, yours, very cordially,*

In reply (1.4.36.) Gaisberg informed Rosenthal that the coupling could in no way be changed as it had already been announced in the May Supplement and that the studio would be reserved for Rosenthal's preferred time.

By the end of April Rosenthal was feeling let down over several issues. He had by now obviously received a letter from Gaisberg - the copy is unfortunately missing from the EMI archives - which not only confirmed the loss of the Chopin *Waltz in A flat* due to the defective master but also explained that the *Nocturne in E flat* could not be issued as it had failed the standard wear test. Perhaps Gaisberg also gave a reason why the *Chant polonais* could not be used. Certainly by the time Rosenthal had settled into the Park Lane Hotel in preparation for his marathon "historic recitals" he was in rebellious mood.

30th April 1936

I hoped for your presence at my Beethoven recital. Alas, you were not there!

I beg you to read these lines in a perfectly friendly spirit, as they are written. The facts, which underlie are grievous, not the sentiments.

Last time I prolonged my staying in London for a certain time, in order to get - at last - some records. I ordered a Bosendorfer Grand, I had a tuner-technician with me, who watched every alteration of the piano. Briefly said on[e] cannot take a matter more seriously than I did in this exceptional case. The effect was brilliant! You flattered me immensely by writing me that you never heard better records and if you may pass them without my examination!

Now, there are different kinds of excellency. The discs may be acustically and musically perfect. But they can be nevertheless a failure pianistically This can only be judged by a high rank pianist but it is most important for the player. I therefore asked you to send me the discs to Vienna and you agreed to do so. But here begann something which looked frightfully like an unwilling and accidental negligence. It took an immense time to send the discs. I could not wait indefinitely, therefore appointed my wife, one of the most musical critics of this world, to judge them. She telegraphed me to Yugoslavia, where I concertized, that never she heard such wonderful discs. And I gave at once permission to sell those records.

*We had the Nocturne Op.9/2 in E flat, the Chant polonais in G
major from a former epoque, [i.e. an earlier session] three
Mazurkas, Valse in C sharp minor and A flat major to be coupled
with the Chant polonais, my Papillons and my Strauss Fantasia
which you said you could free.   Suddenly I heard that the whole
output dwindles down to one disc; Valse Op.42 & 3 Preludes.*

*Now I am justified to ask: How is it possible that all the other
discs were destroyed. I spent much money (around 5 guineas a day,
my rooms alone cost 3 guineas daily). The rich and noble
Grammophone Company should give me some satisfaction for such a
loss of time and prestige. Think of it: you handle my discs so
carelessly that you are reduced to advertise in my own recital
<u>Edwin Fischer</u> and <u>A. Cortot.</u> This is the support the <u>GC</u>
[Gramophone Company] <u>HMV gives me</u>!*

*It would be only fair to present me with a substantial check for
my "servaux artistiques". And I ask you besides permission to play
into the Agency in Vienna, for which purpose you should send me
with enough discs to cover my pieces. They will be sure able to
manage the thing, at least they will look out, not to destroy my
best discs!*

Expecting your immediate and friendly answer,

I remain, yours very sincerely,

*PS: I gave 5 guineas daily in playing my pieces in Vienna and not
     in London."*

Exactly what happened to the planned Mazurka coupling as listed in Gaisberg's letter of 9th March 1936 is not known. It would appear that one side, the *Mazurka No.31 in A flat, Op.50/2*, (2EA 2566-1) suffered some kind of technical mishap for, as mentioned in the comments to Session Four, the title had to be re-recorded in Sessions Six and Nine. There seems little doubt, however, that it was the advertising of records by other pianists at Rosenthal's recital which prompted this justifiable outburst, in particular recordings by Cortot. Rosenthal strongly disliked Cortot's playing which he regarded to be so technically unsound as to be laughable.

Gaisberg gave Rosenthal the benefit of an "immediate" answer.

1st May 1936

Thank you for your letter of April 30th. I can appreciate your disappointment - that is natural enough, but you seem to think the record business is a very simple affair. Actually, I can assure you it is most complicated. If so many records were spoilt during your last recording in London, how many more would have failed if this work had been undertaken in Vienna, where we simply cannot guarantee good results in this class of recording.

I will admit we were particularly unfortunate in losing so many of your records, but a number of factors combined to bring this about and it is no use crying over spilt milk. The experience gained is valuable and will help us obtain better results the next time we tackle this.

I do not see how we can finance your stay over here for this purpose. You are a partner with us in presenting to the public a series of your piano works. We have to capitalise the factory work, stocks and the selling and our Company think they contribute sufficient towards this venture by so doing.

I can only say how very sorry I am about our failure and assure you that I would not undertake to again attempt this recording, if I did not expect satisfactory results this time.

I will be present at your next Recital. I cannot promise to come to them all, as this is my busiest time of the year during the evenings.

Yours sincerely,

Judging from the tone of Rosenthal's reply the pianist had been quickly mollified. It seems quite possible that Gaisberg had telephoned Rosenthal at the Park Lane Hotel in order to clear the air and, perhaps, explain the complications and risks involved in getting a finished shellac disc from a wax master. Certainly the invigorating breeze of a new start is evident in Rosenthal's repertoire suggestions for the next two sessions; besides the two lost titles, of which he had been so particularly fond, there were also some interesting new ideas as well as some familiar friends including, of course, his own *Papillons*.

3rd May 1936

> *There was some healing oil on my wounds when you told me that my Strauss Fantasy remained intact and arrangements with Lindstroem... are perfected. You would do me the greatest favour in giving order to perfect [manufacture] this disc as quickly as possible.*
> *There is hardly a better advertisement for me than this piece composed and played by yours cordially devoted.*
>
> *For the new essays I recommend:*
> 1. *Valse in C sharp minor, Op.64/2 Chopin*
>   *Chant polonais in G major   Chopin-Liszt*
>
> 2. *Papillons Moriz Rosenthal*
>   *Valse Op.64/1 in D flat Chopin*
>
> 3. *Aufforderung zum Tanz Weber*
>
> 4. *Mazurka   Chopin   (each side*
>   *2 Mazurkas   3 minutes)*
>
> 5. *Etude Op.25/11*
>   *Etudes Op.10/1 & 5*   (* if Lindstroem/Parlophone permit)*
>
> 6. *Fantasy-Impromptu in C sharp minor Chopin*
>   *Tarantella, Op.43   Chopin.*
>   *and some other works?*
>
> *...Do answer as soon as possible to your cordially devoted,*

Gaisberg, receptive to all Rosenthal's suggestions, once again brings up the subject of Schumann's *Papillons*.

4th May 1936

Thank you for your letter of May 3rd. I note the programme you wish to record and will set our plans accordingly. I am very disappointed that we are not to have the Schumann "Papillon" or some Schumann work. I think you are making a serious omission in not giving us this, as we have had many enquiries for it. People seem to associate this with your name, although I notice it is not included in your current programmes.

I should also like to include the Soiree de Vienne (Schubert-Liszt) as well as Invitation to the Valtz (Weber) which I see you propose.

We have now cleared up the matter of the New carneval de Vienne and I will let you hear it when you come to the studios...

With kindest regards,

This was the kind of news Rosenthal had been waiting for. He also displays Gaisbergian qualities of patience and understanding in dealing with the repeated demand for him to record Schumann's *Papillons* while he warms to the idea of *Soirées de Vienne* - to the extent of advising Gaisberg that it would have to be accommodated on two sides of a ten inch disc.

5th May 1936

Im exceedingly happy about the resurrection of my Carneval de Vienne. Thanks! I think we should scratch out the "new" and have simply: Carneval de Vienne...

Now, Papillons cannot be demanded as composed by Schumann. I never played this piece by Schumann and one evidently wishes my own Papillons. Perhaps they escaped destruction? They were played at an earlier date and want repeated tryings. Soirées de Vienne I could easily try, but it takes 5 minutes.

Shall we not couple that Chant polonais with Valse in C sharp minor?...

With my kindest regards,

Yours sincerely,

Rosenthal's revised version of his *Carneval de Vienne* was eventually published as "New".

Having completed his mammoth seven recital survey of the piano literature from Bach to Brahms Rosenthal disported himself in similar fashion in the recording studio - four arduous afternoons within six days. Gaisberg too did his utmost, ensuring that each title was processed and samples made available as quickly as possible, thus enabling quick decisions to be made as to whether re-takes were necessary. This accounts for the first three titles being identical in the first three sessions.

Of the repertoire ideas Rosenthal put forward in his letter of the 3rd May 1936 Gaisberg obviously again steered clear of the Chopin Etudes, previously recorded for Parlophone, while the Chopin *Fantasy-Impromptu* and *Tarantella* plus Weber's *Invitation to the Dance* were forgotten.

SESSION SIX: 20.5.36
                                No.3 Studio, Abbey Road, London.
                                Bosendorfer

2EA 2565-2   Chopin: Valse No.7 in C sharp minor, Op.64/2

2EA 2566-2   Chopin: Mazurka No.31 in A flat, Op.50/2

2EA 3640-1)   Chopin: Nocturne No.2 in E flat, Op.9/2
2EA 3640-2)

2EA 3641-1   Chopin: Nocturne No.8 in D flat, Op.27/2

COMMENTS

The Chopin Valtz was a retake of a title from Session Four. So too, for reasons still not fully known, as mentioned previously, was the Mazurka No.31. This was erroneously given a new matrix number (2EA 3642-1) and only later renumbered 2EA 2566-2. The additional and unannounced Mazurka No.44, Op.67/1 contained on 2EA 2566-1 was not included in subsequent retakes of 2EA 3642/2EA 2566.

Nothing from this session was published.

SESSION SEVEN: 21.5.36.
                                  No.3 Studio, Abbey Road, London.
                                  Bosendorfer

2EA 2565-3   Chopin: Valse No.7 in C sharp minor, Op.64/2

2EA 3640-3   Chopin: Nocturne No.2 in E flat, Op.9/2

2EA 3641-2)   Chopin: Nocturne No.8 in D flat, Op.27/2
2EA 3641-3)

OEA 3643-1   Mendelssohn: Song without words in A, Op.62/6 (Spring song)

COMMENTS
    Again, nothing from this session was published. The subsequent retakes of the Chopin titles in Session Eight were those which were approved for publication. There is no indication why the Mendelssohn Spring Song, presumably a potential coupling for Rosenthal's Papillons, was not published.

SESSION EIGHT: 22.5.36
                                   No.3 Studio, Abbey Road, London.
                                   Bosendorfer

2EA 2565-4   Chopin: Valse No.7 in C sharp minor, Op.64/2

2EA 3640-4   Chopin: Nocturne No.2 in E flat, Op.9/2

2EA 3641-4)   Chopin: Nocturne No.8 in D flat, Op. 27/2
2EA 3641-5)

OEA 3644-1   Rosenthal: Papillons

OEA 3645-1   Schubert: Moment musical, No.3 in F minor, D.780

2EA 3646-1   Chopin-Liszt-Rosenthal: Chant polonais No.1 in G (Maiden's
                                   Wish)

COMMENTS

This proved the most productive of the May 1936 sessions. All four Chopin titles were approved:
    2EA 2565-4 and 2EA 3646-1 were allocated the coupling number DB 2923
    2EA 3640-4 and 2EA 3641-5 were allocated the coupling number DB 2926
though these were never published in the UK and make their first appearance on APR 7002.

Rosenthal's attempts to record Papillons continued with the allocation of a new matrix number. This first take was at first marked as accepted by the artist though Rosenthal obviously underwent a change of heart. It was subsequently re-recorded to his satisfaction in Session Eleven. Schubert's Moment musical in F minor - another possible coupling to Papillons? - was satisfactorily recorded in Session Ten.

SESSION NINE: 25.5.36
                                   No.3 Studio, Abbey Road, London.
                                   Bosendorfer

2EA 2566-3   Chopin: Mazurka No.31 in A flat, Op.50/2

OEA 3647-1)   Schubert-Liszt: Soirées de Vienne, No.6 Valse caprice in A Pt.1
OEA 3647-2)

OEA 3648-1)   Schubert-Liszt: Soirées de Vienne, No.6 Valse caprice in A Pt.2
OEA 3648-2)

2EA 3649-1)   Chopin Mazurkas: "Op.68/8" & No.44 in G, Op.67/1
2EA 3649-2)

COMMENTS
         The Chopin Mazurka No.31 was recorded as 2EA 3642-2 and only later changed to 2EA 2566-3 (see comments to Sessions Four & Six). This was published as part of DB 2773.

         The first takes of the Schubert-Liszt (OEA 3647 & 3648) were approved and allocated the coupling number DA 1510. It was unpublished in the UK and appears for the first time on APR 7002.

         Rosenthal disapproved of only the Op.67 Mazurka of 2EA 3649-1 though 2EA 3649-2 was rejected outright. The erroneous opus number "Op.68/8" in all probability refers to Op.68/2, the Mazurka No.47 in A minor.

Rosenthal, aged 73, had completed the most arduous and concentrated spell of work he ever undertook for EMI. Surely now his (and Gaisberg's) efforts would be rewarded.

CHAPTER FOUR
"Very grammophonesque and prepared"

Back in Vienna little more than a week passed before Rosenthal recommenced the train of correspondence. Still in his flowing, copper-plate hand and now approaching Gaisberg as a friend and confidant, these letters are far less demanding, often solicitous, inclined towards informality, sprinkled with chit-chat and occasionally laced with shafts of his famous wit. Gaisberg remains the efficient business man and resists the offered embrace.

3rd June 1936

> *You can easily imagine, how anxious I am to hear about my new records! Would you kindly write me, how I succeeded? On June 1st there came out [i.e. released] my Strauss-Fantasia, which interests me violently. Do send me a few discs of this record...*
>
> *With kindest regards and greetings,*
>
> *Yours, very sincerely,*

Having secured the release of the *Carneval de Vienne* title from Parlophone, thus enabling the issue of the new version recorded at Session Five, Gaisberg made sure that the processing of the waxes recorded during Sessions Six to Nine was done with all possible speed in an attempt to keep some momentum to the release of Rosenthal's records. His favourable initial reaction crossed in the post with Rosenthal's opening shot.

4th June 1936

> *We are now receiving from the factory the samples of the records which you made during your stay in London. I think that among them there will be some very beautiful and successful records.*
>
> *To send this large number of pressings to Vienna will take time and it will be weeks before we can get a decision from you. Could you not trust us to listen to these records and approve them? In the meantime we will send you the samples, so that you can confirm our selections. I presume you would like them sent to Vienna.*
>
> *As soon as they arrive, would you hear them at the Kartnerstrasse shop, because that is the only place where I am certain there will be a gramophone good enough to give a faithful reproduction and on which you can pass judgement.*
>
> *With kind regards, I remain,*
>
> *Yours sincerely,*

Just days later Gaisberg was in receipt of Rosenthal's enquiry.

8th June 1936

> *Thank you for your letter of the 3rd. The samples of your records will be shipped this week and I am certain that you are going to like them. I have heard them and am very pleased. I want to get from you as quickly as possible, your selection of masters and for this purpose I think it best for you to hear the records in the shop at Kartnerstrasse 30. I am therefore sending them direct to Mr. Klopfer at the shop and asking him to notify you when they arrive and play them over for you...*
>
> *With kind regards, I remain,*
>
> *Yours sincerely,*

Rosenthal felt that he could quite easily assess the artistic merit of his records in the comfort of his own home though in all other respects he was most amenable, even to the point of suggesting that Gaisberg be near at hand during the summer vacation.

9th June 1936

> *Of course, you may begin to examine the new discs. I know you understand them in the highest degree. For purely pianistic reasons I would like to hear them before they are submitted to the large public. As said: I have the utmost confidence in your judgement, therefore I will not examine them otherwise than from my pianistic point of view. Therefore, I may try them even at [on a] less perfect grammophone as the pianistic state will not be altered by the place I hear the discs.*
>
> *Now, be a true friend and send me the new discs as quickly as you can, but send me also the New Carneval de Vienne, as I would so much like to hear it and to tell the Radio people to play it. What about the Chant polonais, the Papillons = Butterflies (!) and the two Nocturnes, which should be of perfect ornamental work, but perhaps are not? In October I may come to London in order to play some popular pieces into your splendid grammophones.*
>
> *I spent a wonderful day in Paris with my friend Paderewski...I played for him this Habanera I composed and he burst out in enthusiastic words and applause. He told me: you may make more money by this piece than through a concert tour. I want an excellent poët to find words for my melodies and would like to know if I can expect __financially__ in this instance something like the lions share. This is the best way to be lionised!*
> *Why don't you come to Bad Gastein in Austria? It is the most charming spot in Europe for July and August (3300 feet high). Would be charmed to have you there.*
>
> *Yours, most sincerely,*

Having received Gaisberg's letter of the 8th, Rosenthal decides to put himself out and visit Kartnerstrasse after all - if only the records would arrive.

<u>12th June 1936</u>

> *Am most happy to hear from you that my records please you. I feel sure that your judgement is of great importance and hope the discs will do me honour pianistically. I will await Mr. Klopfers call and go to his shop immediately...*
>
> *Ever so many greetings,*
>
> *From yours sincerely,*

Safe in the knowledge that the test pressings had been despatched Gaisberg looses little time in badgering Rosenthal for some decisions.

<u>22nd June 1936</u>

> *I hope to hear from you very soon that the records have arrived, but please remember that transportation requires time and you must have patience until they arrive. Please let me have your report immediately you have heard the records, as my hands are tied until I receive this from you.*
>
> *I note Mr. Paderewski's enthusiasm for your Habanera and I am looking forward to the time when I can hear you play it.*
>
> *The New Carneval de Vienne has met with an enthusiastic reception and samples have been sent to you. Only the other day I heard it played on the radio by the B.B.C..*
>
> *I hope that I shall be able to visit Bad Gastein during the month of August, if the political situation remains undisturbed. I passed through last year and thought it a divine spot.*
>
> *With kind regards,*
>
> *Yours sincerely,*

Shades of the delays and frustrations experienced at the beginning of the year once more begin to loom. Rosenthal writes from the Sacher Hotel at Helenental, Baden bei Wien, though he is poised for Bad Gastein.

26th June 1936

> *I am waiting patiently but I am afraid I will have to go to Bad Gastein in a week or so, as Mrs Rosenthal is very fatigued from her lessons and has an ardent desire for Bad Gastein.*
>
> *Am so glad you may come to Gastein. You say rightly it is a divine spot. If I may look out for nice rooms for you write me and I will do my best to find satisfactory dwellings for you.*
>
> *With kindest regards,*
>
> *Yours, very sincerely,*

In one final letter from the Hotel Sacher Rosenthal lets it be known, in somewhat fanciful terms, that the records have still not arrived. Furthermore he is also disappointed with the *New Carneval de Vienne*, just released. If he *had* been playing the commerical pressing at 75 (rather than 78) rpm the result would certainly have appeared somewhat lack-lustre. He might also have been surprised by his uncharacteristic playing of the final chord. But at least Sir Henry Wood would welcome the record's publication as he was an out and out admirer of Rosenthal's "most masterly and ingenious" manipulation of Johann Strauss's waltz and operetta themes. He was intrigued by "their cleverness, for Rosenthal brings out the melody of one of them with his left hand somewhere in the tenor register and superimposes the melody of *another* up in the treble".

3rd July 1936

> *I heard my Carneval de Vienne on a disc, a friend sent me from London (yours have not yet arrived) and I cannot help thinking that a faster tempo (80 instead of 75)) would add much to the effect of the piece. Can this be done (officially)?*

In 27 years I will celebrate (if favoured by the gods!) my 100th birthday. Around this time the discs I recorded on May 20th-26th 1936 May have arrived in Vienna and will warm my hearth with the distant rays of a splendid past. I wonder how they will sound? In two or three days I am leaving for Badgastein (Villa Mühlbergen)...

With kindest regards,

Yours cordially,

PS: *About my Habanera (indorsed by an artist like Paderewski). I would like to know what I can expect from the H.M.Voice if I give you the exclusive rights for the piece? You did not answer me this question in your last letter!*

8th July 1936

Thank you for your letter of July 3rd. I hope by this time you have received your records since they were sent off three weeks ago. Please let me have your selections as soon as possible.

I told you that shipments would take a long time; this cannot be helped as all kinds of papers, documents, 'Permission of import', Quotas etc must be obtained to import records into Austria.

As to your Habanera, we will of course record it, but you would be better advised to submit it to a music publisher...I will do this for you if you will send me the manuscript.

Hoping you are in the best of health.

Yours sincerely,

It is not known whether the records did arrive before Rosenthal left for Bad Gastein. His detailed criticisms and comments concerning the records made during the four May 1936 sessions are not to be found in the archives though Gaisberg's letter of acknowledgement and the subsequent documentation make the pianist's rejections and acceptances readily apparent.

22nd July 1936

> *Thank you for your notes. I read with great satisfaction that you have approved the majority of the records and we shall now have sufficient to begin issue.*
>
> *I note that you will repeat the Papillon (Rosenthal) in October, as well as the Moment Musical. Also that you have rejected the Mazurka Op.67 in G major because of a finger slip.*
>
> *Hoping that you are in the best of health, I remain,*
>
> *Yours sincerely,*

As will be seen from the comments to Sessions Six to Nine, seven titles received Rosenthal's full approval though of these only the *Mazurka No.31* was published in the UK. There is no one reason why the remaining six, all allocated coupling numbers, remained in limbo. The deteriorating world situation - already troubling Gaisberg, as can be seen from his letter of the 22nd June - allied to Rosenthal's subsequent departure to America might well have been the principal contributory factors. At this stage in the proceedings, however, there is no indication that only a small proportion of the approved sides would be published and then almost entirely in the USA. Certainly Rosenthal, on holiday at the Villa Mühlberger at Bad Gastein, was eagerly anticipating a flood of releases.

25th July 1936

> *I sincerely and earnestly hope that the records approved be [by] me and you will appear very soon at your splendid grammophones! Could you issue some of them (or all of them?) in your September edition [supplement]?*
>
> *I am glad you come to Gmunden! It is a splendid spot and perhaps you will feel [like] coming to Badgastein for a few days, which you can reach in 3 hours (or 4) from Gmunden.*
>
> *Sending you my best wishes and greetings,*
>
> *I remain yours, faithfully,*

Obviously in mellow and relaxed mood as he enjoys the Villa Mühlberger, Rosenthal throws out an open invitation to Gaisberg when he holidays nearby.

15th August 1936

> *I hope you enjoy beautiful Gmunden as much as possible. I was once a frequent visitor of this splendid place. Will we not have the great pleasure to see you at Badgastein?*
>
> *I just finished a Fantasy on Gounods Faust and feel sure it will be most effectiv also for the Grammophone.*
>
> *With best greetings,*
>
> *Yours very cordially,*

Gaisberg ignored the gesture. Rosenthal, not a little hurt, writes in admonishing tones, this time from the Grand Hotel, Carezza al Lago in Italy. He also remains unhappy with the *New Carneval de Vienne* record.

10th September 1936

> *I wrote you to Gmunden, inviting you to come to Badgastein. Now, please look at the enveloppe and see how the letter was neglected.*
>
> *The Carneval de Vienne is not universally accepted with praise and I would be happy to play the original one, which may give better results. I will be in London end of October and beginning of November. Could I make then some records? And what about our Chant polonaise, Nocturnes and so on?*
>
> *Many greetings and wishes from yours, cordially,*

In a letter of amends Gaisberg makes it clear that any unfinished business should be confined to tying-up loose ends rather than embarking upon fresh titles - save, of course, for Schumann's *Papillons*!

16th September 1936

> *Thank you for your letter of September 10th. It was very kind of you to invite me to Badgastein, but I did not have time to make such a long journey.*
>
> *I think we have sufficient records for the time being and we must have a chance to exploit these before imposing more work on you. We might just have one session to make the following repeats to use as couplings for successful recordings in hand:*
>
> > *Papillons (Rosenthal)*
> > *Papillons (Schumann) - this has been specially requested*
> > *Mazurka Op.68 No.8)   1 - 12"*
> > *Mazurka Op.67 No.1)   recording*
> > *Moment musical (Schubert).*
>
> *Hoping you are in the best of health and looking forward to seeing you,*
>
> *Yours sincerely,*

Rosenthal was, however, not in the best of health; plans had to be drastically revised.

29th October 1936

> *About 2 weeks ago I fell ill and on the strong advice of my physicians I had to cancel my english concerts <u>before</u> my american tour. Therefore, alas, I will not come this November to London but go directly on the 'Normandy' to New York...*
>
> *I am looking forward with the greatest interest to play for HMV in returning from USA. Am happy to play my Papillons, Chopin's Mazurkas and so on, what you wish. But the Papillons by Schumann I never played in public and there is some mistake in asking for them by the public. Very likely they mean my piece called identically.*

> *I will write you in time about my returning to Europe and my visiting London and the famous Studio of HMV.*
>
> *With many wishes and greetings,*
>
> *Yours, very cordially,*
>
> *PS: I would love to play the Schumann Concerto and the G minor Concerto by Saint-Saëns with orchestra for HMV.*

In cutting down his work load in order to protect his health Rosenthal was wise to sacrifice the UK in favour of America, scene of many of his greatest triumphs and still, perhaps, the country where he was most keenly appreciated. He must also have been thinking about his future; certainly by now he was being made to feel increasingly uncomfortable in the hostile, anti-Jewish atmosphere of Vienna, as is evident elsewhere in his correspondence with The Gramophone Company, some of which is quoted later.

Naturally the lost opportunity to record Rosenthal in concerto repertoire is to be regretted though the impracticalities of such a venture are self-evident. Besides, Cortot's October 1934 recording of the Schumann concerto had only recently entered the catalogue while the elderly though authoritative Arthur de Greef account of Saint-Saëns's *Second Piano Concerto* was still doing valiant service.

<u>5th November 1936</u>

> *I have your letter of October the 9th and am very sorry to hear that you have been unwell. I hope you are now quite yourself again, and that you will have a very successful concert tour in America.*
>
> *We shall look forward to your return to London when we can carry out the recording of the repeats.*
>
> *Concertos are not big sellers now and it hardly pays with the heavy charges which are involved.*

With kind regards,

Yours sincerely,

The first half of 1937 was given over to his North American tour, a triumphant pilgrimage of many major cities which attracted ecstatic press reviews, some of which were quoted in the opening Profile. The Toronto reviews were matched by the New York reports of Rosenthal's two recitals given in the Town Hall during November and December 1936. After his first recital - which included Beethoven's *Sonata, Op.111*, Chopin and Liszt's *Tarantella e Napoli* - the *New York World-Telegram* greeted him as

> *that master distiller of piano tone (who) with a beautiful nonchalence proceeded to stand a large audience on its collective head...Going in for none of your curlycue gestures that threaten to become a necessary adjunct of piano-playing, Mr. Rosenthal made his fingers, and through them his mind and his heart, do the interpreting...Such gossamer phrases as he unreeled, such glorious tone, such fragilely contrasting colors could only come forth at the behest of an interpretative giant of the instrument.*

At the second recital the *New York Times* review was no less dazzling.

> *His is the commanding style of the past; there are not many artists left who play with such boldness of outline and flair for grandeur. He knows secrets of his own concerning a work such as the Chopin Sonata [B minor, Op.58]. He does not hesitate to play the music with unashamed breadth of feeling. Modern pianists may be more meticulous about details but Mr. Rosenthal's aim is to set forth the essential romantic spirit of the work.*

Buoyed-up by his success, Rosenthal was decidedly in no mood for a session of mere retakes.

1st June 1937

> *You certainly heard from [of] my exceptional success in the USA? Kindly read the press notices and consider that my Manager engaged me for a second tour on higher terms.*

> *There was edited [released] a small Chopin album by your Victor Company which evoked laudatory remarks.*

> *Now: I am concertizing at Huddersfield Oct 25th. On October 27th I leave Europe on the SS Queen Mary. As I worked up some pieces of highest rank and besides finished my Fantasy on Gounod's Faust, I would be most desirous to perform under your supervising around 8 - 10 pieces, shorter ones = 3 - 4 mins, longer ones until, 8 - 10 minutes. Kindly answer this proposition as soon as you can. Dates 21st , 22nd, 23rd afternoons. I will be very grammophonesque and prepared, and hope to reach my best efforts*
>
> *Hoping you are very well,*
>
> *I send you and all friends my best greetings and kindest regards,*
>
> *Yours cordially,*

The album Rosenthal refers to was a four record set (M-388) comprising the eight twelve-inch Chopin sides so far approved. Irving Kolodin, writing in *The New York Sun*, welcomed its release as Rosenthal's "first representative recordings" and noted that

> *there are few pianists of today who command the authentic tradition for the performance of this music...and Rosenthal, who received his training from Joseffy and Liszt, is singularly equipped for its presentation. It is the knowledge of his great art and extraordinary taste that make one willing to listen to such familiar matters as the Preludes in B minor, G and A; eventually to discover that there are still a few words to be said on these subjects.*

Gaisberg, however, was not overkeen to take many new titles from Rosenthal and considered three sessions an unnecessary luxury. Even allowing for the fact that Rosenthal was relatively "unproductive" in the studio - certainly when judged alongside Simon Barere and Alfred Cortot, both of whom were regular visitors to Abbey Road during the mid-30s - two sessions were more than enough to record the necessary retakes plus the latest *Faust* transcription.

4th June 1937

I was very happy to receive your letter of June 1st. I had already heard of your great success in America and I am pleased to see that you intend to return again in October.

We certainly will be able to give you two recording dates as you pass through and we have reserved the afternoons of October 21st and 22nd in our recording studio.

I note that you particularly wish to record your 'Fantasy' on Gounod's Faust. This should be a popular number and meet with good response from the public.

I thank you for your good wishes and hope you will continue in good health.

Yours sincerely,

Rosenthal, in charming, friendly and enthusiastic manner, was immovable.

9th June 1937

Thank you ever so much for your lovely letter!

My train from Vienna to London goes only 3 times weekly. As a matter of fact I would have to wait two days in London until I play for HMV. Therefore I beg you to arrange for me <u>three</u> séances, on 20th, 21st and 22nd October, instead of two. You know how rarely I come to London and that I should derive more artistic benefit at these occasions.

Hoping that you will be able to arrange those 3 séances, where I hope to be at my best,

I remain yours, cordially

PS: ...I would be so thankful if you would send a set of my newer records (Victors Chopin Album) to the Radio in Vienna...and another for myself!

Gaisberg capitulates - though he was eventually to get his own way.

17th June 1937

> Thank you for your letter. As requested, I have booked the studio
> for your recording on October 20th, afternoon, as well as the 21st
> and 22nd.
>
> It is extremely difficult to import records into Austria on account
> of the high duties and prohibitions, but we are sending you one set
> of samples of your recent recordings. Owing to the uncontrolled
> use of records by Radio Stations, we cannot send you a second set
> to supply to them free. I do not know the exact position in
> Austria at the moment, but Mr. Thallmayer of:
> > Osterreischische Columbia Graphophon Agentur A.G....
> will be pleased to make the matter clear if you care to call and
> see him.
>
> Yours sincerely,

    As Rosenthal was about to leave Vienna both men wrote to each other with their latest thoughts on the imminent sessions. It is not clear whether Rosenthal was asking for a fourth session or simply an adjustment of dates. Gaisberg, only too familiar with the problems of getting Rosenthal to hear and approve his records, hit upon what seemed to be an attractive and practical idea.

14th October 1937

> I would bless you, could you give me the afternoon of Oct 19th?
> We can perhaps arrange <u>then</u> for a further séance. Do
> I see you Sunday at the Palladium?
>
> Yours cordially,

14th October 1937

I see that we have recording sessons booked for you on the afternoons of October 20th, 21st and 22nd and it occurs to me that if we change the session on the 20th to the morning and rush through the waxes, it might be possible to get sample pressings by the afternoon of the 22nd, when any necessary repeats could be made.

I am therefore reserving the studio for the morning of the 20th, commencing at 10 o/c. The sessions will then be as follows:

> *October 20th - 10 o/c.*
> *"   21st - 2 o/c.*
> *"   22nd - 2 o/c.*

Looking forward to seeing you, I remain,

Yours sincerely,

Having settled in at the familiar surroundings of the Park Lane Hotel, London, Rosenthal let it be known that he did not relish the prospect of a morning session, not even to faciliate the approval of his recordings.

17th October 1937

I was longtime ill in Vienna and cannot play for you before Oct 20th afternoon. Don't be angry! I was awfully disappointed not to see you at the Palladium, would have saved you a written answer or telephon.

Hoping to hear from you as soon as possible,

I remain faithfully yours,

Apologies for absence and the whittling-down of the planned "séances" to just two sessions were apparently made via the telephone. The agreed new repertoire was now restricted to Rosenthal's latest fantasy and the number of retakes confined to just two ten inch sides. Whether record producer or pianist had consigned the remaining unfinished business to limbo will probably never be known. There emerges a feeling of compromise, even a hint of disagreement; certainly some phrases in Gaisberg's letter, not least "the under-signed" seem somewhat chilly.

19th October 1937

> *We have great pleasure in confirming the arrangements made yesterday for your recording at the end of this week.*
>
> *We have reserved our Studio at No.3 Abbey Road, St. John's Wood, from 2 - 5 pm on the afternoons of Friday and Saturday October 22nd and 23rd. The under-signed will arrive at the Park Lane Hotel at approximately 2 o'clock and take you to the Studio.*
>
> *The final arrangements for the programme are as follows:*
> | | |
> |---|---|
> | *Fantasia on Gounod's Faust* | *2-12" sides* |
> | *Papillons (Rosenthal)* | *1-10" side* |
> | *Mazurka (Chopin)* | *1-10" side* |
>
> *Messrs. Bosendorfer have been requested to send your piano in time for the recording and to have their tuner in attendance.*
>
> *We shall look forward to seeing you on Friday afternoon*
>
> *Yours sincerely,*

In the event Rosenthal's new fantasy was not recorded, unlike his ubiquitous *Papillons*. Along with more Chopin than planned there were also two further attempts at the Schubert *Moment musical in F minor*.

SESSION TEN: 22.10.37.
                                No.3 Studio, Abbey Road, London.
                                Bosendorfer

OEA 3645-2)   Schubert: Moment musical, No.3 in F minor, D.780
OEA 3645-3)

OEA 5504-1)   Chopin: Mazurka No.23 in D, Op.33/2
OEA 5504-2)

OEA 5505-1)   Chopin: Mazurka No.39 in B, Op.63/1
OEA 5505-2)

OEA 5506-1   Chopin: Mazurkas No.44 in G, Op.67/1 & No.16 in A flat, Op.24/3

COMMENTS

    OEA 3645-2 was approved and allocated the coupling number DA 1659 though it was never published.

    OEA 5504-2 & OEA 5505-2 were approved and allocated the coupling number DA 1660 though the record was never issued in the UK.

    The little G major Mazurka No.44 (OEA 5506-1), an obvious Rosenthal favourite which had crept in unannounced into 2EA 2566-1 of Session Four, here receives a "legitimate" take partnered by the equally epigrammatic A flat Mazurka, Op.24/3. It was approved and allocated the coupling number DA 1661 but was never published.

    All four titles appear for the first time in the UK on APR 7002.

SESSION ELEVEN: 23.10.37.
                                No.3 Studio, Abbey Road, London,
                                Bosendorfer

OEA 5506-2)   Chopin: Mazurkas No.16 in A flat, Op.24/3 & No.41 in C sharp
OEA 5506-3)   minor, Op.63/3
                        or Mazurkas No.44 in G, Op.67/1 & No.16 in A flat, Op.24/3

OEA 5507-1   Chopin: Prelude No.13 in F sharp, Op.28

OEA 3644-2)   Rosenthal: Papillons
OEA 3644-3)

COMMENTS

The recording sheets are ambiguous concerning OEA 5506. There is a likelihood that the pairing of the Opp.67/1 & 24/3 Mazurkas (as per take one which was subsequently approved) might have been amended - by accident or design - in the retakes of this session.

OEA 5507-1 was approved and allocated the coupling number DA 1661 though it was never published and appears for the first time on APR 7002.

OEA 3644-3 was approved and allocated the coupling number DA 1659. It is especially ironic that this, the last of twelve attempts made at seven of his eleven sessions for HMV was never published. It appears for the first time on APR 7002.

CHAPTER FIVE
"A kind of triumpf"

Rosenthal never returned to the studios in Abbey Road, London. Engulfed by the maelstrom which culminated in the Second World War, he remained in the United States of America, eventually becoming a citizen of that all-welcoming country. He seems to have withstood the trauma of the loss of his home and a large part of his possessions with remarkable equanimity though his financial situation was precarious and he toured incessantly throughout America in a somewhat desperate attempt to remain solvent. In determining the results of his last two recording sessions Rosenthal's spasmodic letters consequently come from all corners of the United States. The first, from New York's Hotel Hamilton, is preoccupied with his financial concerns. (The opening foray is a reference to the previously mentioned RCA Chopin album, M-338.)

6th February 1938

> *Your representative in New York, Victor, edited [issued] my interpretations of the immortel works by Chopin in shape of an album, which enjoyed a stormy vogue. From different people I heard that the album continues to be sold out.*
>
> *I must express some astonishment not having heard from you, neither the HMV nor the Victor Co about this happy occurence. More plainly spoken: a year about has elapsed since the blessed birthday of this album and I have not got a cent and not even an account. You would do me a favour to answer this without delay, as I am leaving for the coast and will be continuously on the voyage. I had here a sensational success. The whole press writes in superlatives and the public has filled Carnegie Hall at my last concert.*
>
> *It comes to me that you should be so kind as to send my royalties c/o Guarantee Trust Co., New York, Fifth Avenue and 44th Street. Kindly write me also, if you would consent I should play into your Victor [i.e. record for RCA Victor which at this time still remained closely connected with The Gramophone Company] in April or wait until I am again at London? How did turn out the last series? How came out the Papillons? Dont forget entirely that at my age I must not wait unneccessarily for such joys of life as good records, the help of a dear friend, and so on.*
>
> *With affectionate greetings,*
>
> *Yours cordially,*

Keen to clear up all outstanding business, Gaisberg again sought permission to pass the records without "troubling" the artist.

16th February 1938

> *I am very happy to receive your beautiful letter from New York and to know that you are having continued success with your recitals. I have also been reading the musical papers from America and am very pleased how universally they give you full honours.*

> *Your last records are successful, but we have withheld issue until you could hear them, as we know how strict you are. However, if you give me permission to pass them, I will see that they are recommended for issue both here and in America.*
>
> *As you know, the royalties from the Victor Company are always six months in arrears, because at the end of each semester, it takes two or three months to obtain the figures from all their far flung selling organisations. We now have the figures of the Victor sales for the half year ended 30th June 1937 and these will be included in the statement which you receive for Gramophone sales to 31st December 1937. These statements should be ready about the middle of March...*
>
> *I do not think there is any urgency for you to record in America. We should much prefer to make records in London when you are passing through, as we obtain our best results here.*
>
> *Wishing you every success and continued good health, I remain,*
>
> *Yours sincerely,*

Rosenthal's financial plight grew more pressing. Writing from the Hotel Ansonia in New York he sounded a desperate note.

12th June 1938

> *Allow me to beg you again not to send monies to my Viennese address! It would go astray!*
>
> *My correct address is:*
>   *Guarantee Trust Co.*
>   *5 Avenue Branch, New York.*
>   *account: Moriz Rosenthal.*
>
> *I may remain a longer time at New York and the US. Could you not arrange for some (interesting) records for me with Victor?...*

> *When are my dollars due? I am cut off from my Viennese Bancs.*
>
> *Sending you my best wishes and greetings,*
>
> *Yours very cordially,*

In a brief letter of 23rd June Gaisberg was able to assure the pianist that his royalty cheque was being prepared and that it would be sent to the New York address. But there was some bad news.

> *We have so many records in reserve just now which will become available to the Victor Company, that there is no immediate necessity of recording.*
>
> *With kind regards,*
>
> *Yours sincerely,*

In what is undoubtedly the most moving letter of the entire exchange of correspondence between Moriz Rosenthal and Fred Gaisberg, the pianist writes from the Shoreland Hotel, Chicago, explaining his recent preoccupation with money matters. While he refrains from commiting himself one way or the other regarding the approval of his last records by proxy, he is keenly aware that something need be done concerning an imminent important event in his career.

6th July 1938

> *There was one important reason for having asked you twice, to send me my fees to N.York. There is a certain party in Vienna, who spys around and confiscates monies if possible. Also a letter to Vienna or at a wrong address might have caused loss of the whole amount.*
>
> *So I was trying to come out of danger. I feel sure, you did not misunderstand my repeated writing and I declare that I would gladly entrust you and your Company with millions, if I only had them.*

As to the records, I feel very sad that my last London discs did not yet appear. Dont you think the Papillons would please the public at large and be a kind of triumpf for me and the great Company, you preside. Do me the favour, dear friend and put your mighty word in the balance for an early appearance.

About new Victor Records : they are still the best in the USA and as on Nov 13th 1938 is the fiftieth anniversary of my first debut in New York and USA (13th of Nov 1888) and I celebrate this date by a concert at Carnegie Hall, I would be happy to play some records in connection with this celebration. Could you write to Victor and order some nice records?

Believe me, dear Mr. Gaisberg,

Yours very faithfully,

Rex Palmer, head of the International Artistes Department, replied on behalf of Gaisberg who was away "on the continent". He injected some momentum into the proceedings realising that the records must be made available to RCA in connection with Rosenthal's jubilee.

12th July 1938

...We have sent your royalties to New York as you requested and quite understand your desire that they should not be sent to Vienna. I confirm that we shall continue to send them to New York in future, unless you advise us to the contrary.

We have been holding the records you made last November for you to hear and approve on your next visit to London, but as this seems indefinite, we are sending copies to the Victor Company so that you can pass them in America.

We have reminded the Victor Company of your Anniversary concert on November 13th and if they desire any additional records in connection with this, they will no doubt discuss the matter with you.

With kindest regards,

Yours sincerely,

True to their word, on the same day The Gramophone Company advised RCA of the titles Rosenthal had recorded in London in November 1938 and that copies were being sent to them for the pianist's approval. It also notified RCA of Rosenthal's desire to make more records. In reply RCA's Charles O'Connell felt that it would not be necessary "to ask Mr. Rosenthal to make additional titles here, as you have been good enough to supply us quite generously with recorded piano literature".

On the 11th August 1938 RCA advised Rosenthal that to date they had not received his records from London but as soon as they arrived his approval would be sought in order that some of them could be released in time for his Jubilee Concert. Aware of how little time remained before the 13th November, Rosenthal enclosed a copy of this letter with what appears to have been his last direct contact with Fred Gaisberg, written from the Antlers Hotel in Colorado Springs.

23rd August 1938

> *Enclosed a letter from Victor. It would be of greatest importance for me to have the new records. On the contrary I would feel it as a <u>real damage</u> not to get the new records in shortest time to Camden [RCA's recording and manufacturing base]. Do me the favour, dear friend, to send them <u>as soon as possible</u>. It will be beneficial to me and very likely to Victor.*
>
> *Many thanks, from your devoted,*

A few weeks later Rex Palmer, received a worried letter from Rosenthal, recently returned to the Hotel Shoreland, Chicago.

5th September 1938

> On July 12th 1938 you wrote me you will send my October [1937]
> records to your Victor Company. I sincerely hope they will reach
> Camden in good shape, but I am very unhappy about the very slow
> adagio tempo they indulge in. It is high time, to avail ourselves
> of my Papillons for instance and the other records, as my Jubilee
> Concert approaches....Please send them as quick as possible!...
>
> Yours sincerely,

Gaisberg was back in the country to pen his last replies to Rosenthal.

6th September 1938

> Thank you for your letter of 23rd August. Your records were
> despatched to the Victor Company on August 18th, so the parcel
> should certainly be in their hands by this time.
>
> Hoping you are in the best of health, I remain,
>
> Yours sincerely,

16th September 1938

> In reply to your letter of September 5th, your records should
> now be in the possession of the Victor Company. It is well known
> that it takes a long time for records to arrive, on account of
> Customs delays...
>
> With kindest regards and all good wishes,
>
> Yours sincerely,

With that the correspondence between Moriz Rosenthal and Fred Gaisberg came to an inconclusive end. Of the six approved sides emanating from the two October 1937 sessions none were ever published in the UK and only two in America, just in time for Rosenthal's Jubilee Concert in New York.

In a bizarre even cruel twist the recordings Rosenthal made during his last two sessions, arguably the finest of all his gramophone performances, have for the most part remained unpublished for almost fifty years. His incomparable Chopin *Mazurka* readings recall the review of his February 1934 London recital, the occasion at which Gaisberg first met the pianist, when *The Times* noted that Rosenthal's Mazurka performances were "especially entrancing for the way in which the details were morticed together into perfect miniature forms". No less remarkable is Rosenthal's interpretaion of the Chopin *Prelude No.13*, at once valedictory and prophetic. Arthur Hedley, that noted Chopin scholar, once recalled that one "hard-bitten music critic confessed that, as he listened to Rosenthal playing (this Prelude in F sharp), he felt with emotion that it was the music of a vanished age, heard as in a shell that had been cast up on the shore of time". Certainly the performance, full of inner vision, has an indescribable, otherworldly beauty about it.

Some general letters from Rosenthal to The Gramophone Company were to follow, routine matters concerned mostly with royalty statements and earnings, written in a noticeably faltering hand. Even such mundane exchanges as these were soon impeded by the growing intensity of the Second World War. By 1941 regulations obliged Rosenthal to provide details of "nationality and immigration" before he could receive his dues while in the following year government restrictions were tightened still further so that he was compelled to prove that he was "a non-enemy alien". Such were the last, sad dealings Moriz Rosenthal had with The Gramophone Company.

Rosenthal's HMV recordings were not his last. RCA Victor provided him with studio time in 1939 and again in 1942 when he was eighty. Despite an occasional fleeting glimpse of magic these recordings are little more than the angry roar of an old lion, one who is no longer leader of the pack, though they do bring us full circle. Fourteen years earlier Rosenthal made his first published record at RCA, his *Blue Danube Fantasy* which began our story.

Rosenthal's belated conversion to the gramophone was surprisingly convincing and comparatively prolific. Naturally we regret that the unbridled virtuosity of Rosenthal's earlier years was never captured on disc but we can be grateful that, despite the odds, Rosenthal and The Gramophone Company did eventually coincide. Rosenthal the musing, reflective philosopher, the refined, keyboard poet is captured to perfection in his series of HMV recordings. They contribute a key chapter in the remarkable history of the pianists from the golden age.

DISCOGRAPHY A
Repertoire analysis

NB: All surviving titles included on APR 7002 are indicated in **bold type**.

CHOPIN
Etudes:
   in F, Op.25/2   **2EA 1365-1**   Session Three
   in G flat, Op.10/5 (Black Key)   **OEA 1369-1)**
                                           OEA 1369-2)   Session Three
                                           OEA 1369-3)
   Nouvelle etude No.3 in A flat   **2EA 1365-1**   Session Three
Mazurkas:
   No.16 in A flat, Op.24/3   **OEA 5506-1**   Session Ten
                                           OEA 5506-2)   Session Eleven*
                                           OEA 5506-3)
   No.23 in D, Op.33/2   OEA 5504-1)   Session Ten
                                           OEA 5504-2)
   No.25 in B minor, Op.33/4   2EA 2567-1   Session Five
   No.31 in A flat, Op.50/2   **OEA 1366-1**   Session Three
                                           2EA 2566-1   Session Four
                                           2EA 2566-2   Session Six
                                           2EA 2566-3   Session Nine
   No.39 in B, Op.63/1   OEA 5505-1)   Session Ten
                                           OEA 5505-2)
   No.41 in C charp minor, Op.63/3   OEA 5506-2)   Session Eleven*
                                           OEA 5506-3)
   No.44 in G, Op.67/1   **2EA 2566-1**   Session Four
                                           2EA 3649-1)   Session Nine
                                           2EA 3649-2)
                                           OEA 5506-1   Session Ten
                                           OEA 5506-2)   Session Eleven*
                                           OEA 5506-3)
   "Opp 50/2 & 24/3"   OEA 1367-1)   Session Three*
                                           OEA 1367-2)
   "Op.68/8"   2EA 3649-1)   Session Nine*
                                           2EA 3649-2)
Nocturnes:
   No.2 in E flat, Op.9/2   2EA 1359-1)   Session Two
                                           2EA 1359-2)
                                           2EA 2564-1   Session Four
                                           2EA 3640-1)   Session Six
                                           2EA 3640-2)
                                           2EA 3640-3   Session Seven
                                           2EA 3640-4   Session Eight

No.8 in D flat, Op.27/2	2EA 3641-1	Session Six
	2EA 3641-2)	Session Seven
	2EA 3641-3)	
	2EA 3641-4)	Session Eight
	2EA 3641-5)	
Preludes, Op.28:		
No.3	OEA 1363-1)	Session Three
	OEA 1363-2)	
	2EA 2562-1)	Session Four
	2EA 2562-2)	
No.6	2EA 2562-1)	Session Four
	2EA 2562-2)	
No.7	OEA 1363-1)	Session Three
	OEA 1363-2)	
	2EA 2562-1)	Session Four
	2EA 2562-2)	
No.11	OEA 1363-1)	Session Three
	OEA 1363-2)	
No.13 in F sharp	**OEA 5507-1**	Session Eleven
No.23	OEA 1363-1)	Session Three
	OEA 1363-2)	
Valses:		
No.3 in A minor, Op.34/2	2EA 1368-1	Session Three
No.5 in A flat, Op.42	2B 6007-1)	Session One
	2B 6007-2)	
	2EA 1358-1)	Session Two
	2EA 1358-2)	
	2EA 2561-1)	Session Four
	2EA 2561-2)	
No.7 in C sharp minor, Op.64/2	2EA 1364-1)	Session Three
	2EA 1364-2)	
	2EA 2565-1	Session Four
	2EA 2565-2	Session Six
	2EA 2565-3	Session Seven
	2EA 2565-4	Session Eight
CHOPIN-LISZT		
Chant polonais No.1 in G (Maiden's Wish)	2B 6006-1)	Session One+
	2B 6006-2)	
	2EA 1355-1)	Session Two
	2EA 1355-2)	
	2EA 3646-1	Session Eight+
MENDELSSOHN		
Song without words, Op.62/6 (Spring song)	OEA 3643-1	Session Seven*

ROSENTHAL
   Papillons

	2B 6008-1	Session One
	OEA 1357-1	Session Two
	OEA 1357-2)	
	OEA 1357-3)	Session Three
	OEA 1357-4)	
	OEA 2563-1)	Session Four
	OEA 2563-2)	
	OEA 2563-3)	Session Five
	OEA 2563-4)	
	OEA 3644-1	Session Eight
	OEA 3644-2)	Session Eleven
	OEA 3644-3)	

SCHUBERT
   Moment musical No.3 in F minor

	OEA 3645-1	Session Eight
	OEA 3645-2)	Session Ten
	OEA 3645-3)	

SCHUBERT-LISZT
   Soirées de Vienne, No.6 *Part One*

	OEA 3647-1)	Session Nine
	OEA 3647-2)	

   Soirées de Vienne, No.6 *Part Two*

	OEA 3648-1)	Session Nine
	OEA 3648-2)	

J.STRAUSS-ROSENTHAL
   New Carneval de Vienne *Part One*

	2B 6004-1	Session One
	2EA 1356-1)	Session Two
	2EA 1356-2)	
	2EA 2568-1	Session Five

   New Carneval de Vienne *Part Two*

	2B 6005-1)	Session One
	2B 6005-2)	
	2EA 2569-1	Session Five

* It is not possible to verify the accuracy of this title. Details are as per recording sheets.

+ Recorded in Rosenthal's own distinctive version of this title

DISCOGRAPHY B
78 rpm Published Titles
Matrix Numbers with Coupling Numbers

NB: This discography confines itself to the titles published in 78 rpm form.

	UK/HMV	USA/RCA	Japan/RCA
2EA 2561-1 CHOPIN Valse No.5 in A flat, Op.42	DB 2772	14299 M 338	D 836
2EA 2562-2 Chopin Preludes, Op.28 - Nos. 6,3 & 7	DB 2772	14300 M 338	D 836
2EA 2565-4 Chopin Valse No.7 in C# minor, Op.64/2	DB 2923*	14299 M 338	D 1396
2EA 2566-1 Chopin Mazurkas No.31 in A flat, Op.50/2) No.44 in G, Op.67/1)		14304 M 338	
2EA 2566-3 Chopin Mazurka No.31 in A flat, Op.50/2	DB 2773	14298	D 924
2EA 2567-1 Chopin Mazurka No.25 in B minor, Op.33/4	DB 2773	14298 M 338	D 924
2EA 2568-1 J.Strauss-Rosenthal New Carneval Pt 1	DB 2836	11-8175	
2EA 2569-1 J.Strauss-Rosenthal New Carneval Pt 2	DB 2836	11-8175	
2EA 3640-4 Chopin Nocturne No.2 in E flat, Op.9/2	DB 2926*	14297 M 338	D 871
2EA 3641-5 Chopin Nocturne No.8 in D flat, Op.27/2	DB 2926*	14297 M 338	D 871
OEA 3644-3 Rosenthal Papillons	DA 1659*		

OEA 3645-2
Schubert Moment musical No.3 in F   DA 1659*
        minor, D.780

2EA 3646-1
Chopin-Liszt-Rosenthal Chant polonais   DB 2923*   14300   D 1396
        No.1 in G (Maiden's Wish)   14304
                                                      M 338

OEA 3647-1
Schubert-Liszt Soirée de Vienne No.6 Pt 1 DA 1510*   1854

OEA 3648-1
Schubert-Liszt Soirée de Vienne No.6 Pt 2 DA 1510*   1854

OEA 5504-2
Chopin Mazurka No.23 in D, Op.33/2   DA 1660*   1951

OEA 5505-2
Chopin Mazurka No.39 in B, Op.63/1   DA 1660*   1951

OEA 5506-1
Chopin Mazurkas No.44 in G, Op.67/1
                No.16 in A flat, Op.24/3   DA 1661*

OEA 5507-1
Chopin Prelude No.13 in F#, Op.28   DA 1661*

* HMV coupling number allocated but not used and therefore unissued in the UK.

Titles published by Travis & Emery Music Bookshop:

Bathe, William: A Briefe Introduction to the Skill of Song
Bax, Arnold: Symphony #5, Arranged for Piano for Four Hands by Walter Emery
Burney, Charles: An Account of the Musical Performances in Westminster-Abbey
Burney, Charles: The Present State of Music in France and Italy
Burney, Charles: The Present State of Music in Germany, The Netherlands …
Crimp, Bryan: Dear Mr. Rosenthal … Dear Mr. Gaisberg …
Crimp, Bryan: Solo: The Biography of Solomon
Frescobaldi, Girolamo: D'Arie Musicali per Cantarsi. Primo Libro & Secondo Libro.
Geminiani, Francesco: The Art of Playing the Violin.
Hawkins, John: A General History of the Science and Practice of Music (5 vols.)
Herbert-Caesari, Edgar: The Science and Sensations of Vocal Tone
Herbert-Caesari, Edgar: Vocal Truth
Isaacs, Lewis: Hänsel and Gretel. A Guide to Humperdinck's Opera.
Isaacs, Lewis: Königskinder (Royal Children) A Guide to Humperdinck's Opera.
Lascelles (née Catley), Anne: The Life of Miss Anne Catley.
Mainwaring, John: Memoirs of the Life of the Late George Frederic Handel
Malcolm, Alexander: A Treaty of Music: Speculative, Practical and Historical
Mellers, Wilfrid: Angels of the Night: Popular Female Singers of Our Time
Mellers, Wilfrid: Bach and the Dance of God
Mellers, Wilfrid: Beethoven and the Voice of God
Mellers, Wilfrid: Caliban Reborn - Renewal in Twentieth Century Music
Mellers, Wilfrid: François Couperin and the French Classical Tradition
Mellers, Wilfrid: Harmonious Meeting
Mellers, Wilfrid: Le Jardin Retrouvé, The Music of Frederic Mompou
Mellers, Wilfrid: Music and Society, England and the European Tradition
Mellers, Wilfrid: Music in a New Found Land: … … American Music
Mellers, Wilfrid: Romanticism and the Twentieth Century (from 1800)
Mellers, Wilfrid: The Masks of Orpheus: …… the Story of European Music.
Mellers, Wilfrid: The Sonata Principle (from c. 1750)
Mellers, Wilfrid: Vaughan Williams and the Vision of Albion
Playford, John: An Introduction to the Skill of Musick.
Purcell, Henry et al: Harmonia Sacra … The First Book, [1726]
Purcell, Henry et al: Harmonia Sacra … Book II [1726]
Quantz, Johann: Versuch einer Anweisung die Flöte traversiere zu spielen.
Rastall, Richard: The Notation of Western Music.
Rimbault, Edward: The Pianoforte, Its Origins, Progress, and Construction.
Rubinstein, Anton : Guide to the proper use of the Pianoforte Pedals.
Simpson, Christopher: A Compendium of Practical Musick in Five Parts
Spohr, Louis: Grand Violin School
Tans'ur, William: A New Musical Grammar; or The Harmonical Spectator
Tosi, Pier Francesco: Observations on the Florid Song.
Van der Straeten, Edmund: History of the Violoncello, The Viol da Gamba …
Van der Straeten, Edmund: History of the Violin, Its Ancestors… Vol.1.
Van der Straeten, Edmund: History of the Violin, Its Ancestors… Vol.2.

Travis & Emery Music Bookshop
17 Cecil Court, London, WC2N 4EZ, United Kingdom.
Tel. (+44) 20 7240 2129

© Travis & Emery 2009

www.ingramcontent.com/pod-product-compliance
Lightning Source LLC
Chambersburg PA
CBHW081522160426
43195CB00015B/2474